Unshackling Accountants

Unshackling Accountants

D.R. MYDDELTON

The Institute of Economic Affairs

First published in Great Britain in 2004 by
The Institute of Economic Affairs
2 Lord North Street
Westminster
London sw1p 3lb
in association with Profile Books Ltd

The mission of the Institute of Economic Affairs is to improve public understanding of the fundamental institutions of a free society, with particular reference to the role of markets in solving economic and social problems.

A CIP catalogue record for this book is available from the British Library.

isbn 0 255 36559 4

Many IEA publications are translated into languages other than English or are reprinted. Permission to translate or to reprint should be sought from the Director General at the address above.

Typeset in Stone by MacGuru Ltd
info@macguru.org.uk

Printed and bound in Great Britain by Hobbs the Printers

CONTENTS

THE AUTHOR

D. R. Myddelton was educated at Eton and the Harvard Business School. He is a chartered accountant. Since 1972 he has been Professor of Finance and Accounting at the Cranfield School of Management. He has for many years been a member of the councils of Cranfield University and of the University of Buckingham. He is chairman of the managing trustees of the Institute of Economic Affairs.

Professor Myddelton has written many books and articles, and has contributed to IEA publications on the subjects of tax and inflation. His textbooks include: *The Meaning of Company Accounts* (7th edition, 2000), with Professor Walter Reid; *Essential Management Accounting* (2nd edition, 1993), with M. W. Allen; and *Managing Business Finance* (2000). He has also written *On a Cloth Untrue: Inflation Accounting, The Way Forward* (1984) and *The Power to Destroy: A Study of the British Tax System* (2nd edition, 1994).

FOREWORD

It is a paradox of modern times that financial scandals in our increasingly regulated world are greeted with a cry for more government regulation. Yet such government regulation appears to have done nothing to reduce the propensity for scandals. Indeed, government regulation may have made matters worse: it can prevent market mechanisms of regulation evolving; it can reduce the responsibility of individual professionals and professional bodies; and it can increase moral hazard so that individuals take decisions less aware of and less able to deal with the problems of financial risk.

Hayek addressed this paradox by explaining that clever people will look at the imperfections of the world and try to make the world perfect by ever more rational coordination and design of man's activities. Hence we have the drive to achieve a scandal- and trouble-free financial and corporate world through more government regulation. When a problem arises, such people do not accept the imperfect world as it is; still less do they believe that detailed regulation will make it worse: instead they try to perfect it by more regulation.

Professor Myddelton, in *Unshackling Accountants*, explains how there has been an explosion in accounting regulation in recent decades. This has been driven by the hierarchies of professional bodies, by statutory regulators and by various levels of government. The effect has been to move from a situation where accountants took professional responsibility to ensure that accounts gave 'a true and fair view' to one where specific methods of calculation are laid down by regulatory authorities of various types. There are many problems with this approach. Inappropriate standards can be forced upon the whole profession, giving misleading pictures of companies' affairs; accounts are being asked to perform functions they were not intended to perform, thus lulling investors into a false sense of security; the approach will prevent better accounting methods evolving, and so on.

There are very close analogies between Professor Myddelton's analysis and similar developments in the field of pensions and insurance. There are, at the current time, serious concerns about the solvency of major insurance companies and of pension funds. With regard to the insurance industry, government and its regulators are blaming the antiquated techniques used in insurance companies. Yet these techniques were imposed on insurance companies through various sets of laws and regulations passed in the early 1980s. The use of certain more modern techniques was explicitly discouraged. The use of more sophisticated approaches to insurance accounting altogether was implicitly discouraged by the requirement to conduct expensive investigations to provide reams of information to regulators that often turned out to be useless.

In pension fund accounting, Professor Myddelton mentions the imposition of standards that involve very precise and radical ways of accounting for pension costs. This is one of the many standards to which he draws attention where reasonable people could have different views. There has been wide debate within the actuarial and accounting professions about the standards for accounting for pension costs. There are strong arguments on both sides. Two important points can be made. If the philosophy underlying the standard turns out to be an incorrect one, its uniform imposition could have catastrophic effects on companies and their pension funds – some would argue that it already has. Second, there is no consensus here. If ever there was a need for 'competition' to discover the best way of doing things it is in this area. Yet, for some reason, government and some in professional bodies prefer neat uniformity of processes rather than a framework that can lead to the discovery of the best methods of accounting. Uniformity of process is not necessary to ensure good stewardship. Furthermore, investment analysts are well able to make appropriate adjustments to their company evaluations to provide information to potential investors: indeed, that is their job.

Professor Myddelton makes a strong case for unshackling accountants from the detailed regulation that surrounds them. But that does not mean there would be a 'free for all'. Accounts would have to give 'a true and fair view' and individual professionals would have to indicate that they did so. The profession could still give guidance and suggestions for recommended practice. If an accountant were challenged in law, he would have to justify that his methods provided 'a true and fair view'. It would be clear that accountants could never shelter behind the approaches suggested by their professional body, but the general acceptance and professional integrity of the methods used would be a factor that a court could take into account when judging whether accountants had given 'a true and fair view'. If a particular accounting technique used in practice is not part of the profession's recommended practice but had wide acceptance or a strong intellectual justification, this should not invalidate a set of accounts.

In case it is felt that this is unrealistic or idealistic, it should be noted that this is precisely the approach that has been taken throughout the history of the accounting profession. It is the approach that has led to the evolution of today's sophisticated methods which are necessary for reporting on the financial activities of large and complex companies. Those who wish to take the radically different approach of improving uniformity pioneered in recent years surely need to demonstrate that this has led to less financial scandal, better information and better professional standards.

The views expressed in Hobart Paper 149 are, as in all IEA publications, those of the author and not those of the Institute (which has no corporate view), its managing trustees, Academic Advisory Council or senior staff.

PHILIP BOOTH

Editorial and Programme Director,
Institute of Economic Affairs
Professor of Insurance and Risk Management,
Sir John Cass Business School, City University
April 2004

ACKNOWLEDGEMENTS

I am grateful to the following for commenting on one or more earlier drafts of this paper: Henry Gold, Professor John Grinyer, A. J. Myddelton, Roger Myddelton, Professor David Pendrill, Malcolm Raiser and Professor Peter Watson. I would also like to thank Professor Colin Robinson and Professor Philip Booth for their sympathetic editorial support. I benefited from the constructive criticism of anonymous referees. My thanks also to Sheila Hart, Thea Hughes and Heather Simpkins at Cranfield for their help in finalising the text.

EXECUTIVE SUMMARY

- In law, annual accounts reporting to all shareholders about corporate performance and financial position are not prospectuses inviting people to invest. The main purpose of company accounts is to enable shareholders to monitor the stewardship of managers.

- The generally accepted orthodox approach, using historical cost, emphasises consistent prudent matching of expenses against earned sales revenues. In contrast, standard-setters are now imposing a revolutionary approach aiming to transform accounts into instruments for predicting future cash flows.

- Some people assume that regulators know best and want regulators' views imposed on everyone. But there is no agreement today on what is 'best' in accounting, and even if there were it might not last long. The Accounting Standards Board is using principles which most professional accountants do not accept and which the vast majority of companies find irrelevant.

- The stimulus for accounting regulation has often been so-called 'scandals'. Yet there is little evidence to show that misleading disclosure has caused losses to investors. A non-problem followed by a non-solution: perhaps that sums up the history of accounting standards.

- Accounting standards have increasingly aimed at 'decision usefulness' – assisting potential investors with investment decisions. Fundamental analysis of company accounts is not, however, 'useful' to investors in predicting future profits. Potential investors should use other sources of information.
- As so often when regulation falls short of what it promises, the 'solution' is to reinforce failure by more of the same. Regulators want to avoid blame if things go wrong. They will be risk-averse and have an in-built tendency to over-regulate. Since the publication in 1995 of Hobart Paper 128, *Accountants without Standards?*, the volume of UK accounting standards, including company law, has risen from 800 to 2,000 pages.
- There are various bodies that can be involved with the setting of financial reporting standards. Intervention by different levels of government has almost always been a failure; stock exchanges can produce standards for information provision by traded companies: this has generally been successful, but regulators have taken over much of this role; professional bodies can produce accounting standards to be used by their members.
- Where professional bodies produce standards, they should recognise the subjective nature of accounting and provide 'suggestions' for their members to follow. Government regulators should not be involved in this process.

TABLES

ACRONYMS

Many acronyms are used throughout the text. They are explained below. A glossary follows.

United Kingdom (UK)

ASB	Accounting Standards Board
ASC	Accounting Standards Committee
ASSC	Accounting Standards Steering Committee
CCAB	Consultative Committee of Accountancy Bodies
DTI	Department of Trade and Industry
ED	Exposure Draft (for SSAP)
FRC	Financial Reporting Council
FRED	Financial Reporting Exposure Draft
FRRP	Financial Reporting Review Panel
FRS	Financial Reporting Standard
FRSSE	Financial Reporting Standard for Smaller Entities
FSA	Financial Services Authority
GAAP	Generally Accepted Accounting Practice
ICAEW	Institute of Chartered Accountants in England and Wales
ICAS	Institute of Chartered Accountants of Scotland
LSE	London Stock Exchange
OFR	Operating and Financial Review

SoP	Statement of Principles
SORP	Statement of Recommended Practice
SSAP	Statement of Standard Accounting Practice
STRGL	Statement of Total Recognised Gains and Losses
UITF	Urgent Issues Task Force

United States (USA)

AAA	American Accounting Association
AICPA	American Institute of Certified Public Accountants
APB	Accounting Principles Board
ARB	Accounting Research Bulletin
ARS	Accounting Research Study
ASR	Accounting Series Release
CAP	Committee on Accounting Procedure
FAF	Financial Accounting Foundation
FASB	Financial Accounting Standards Board
FEI	Financial Executives Institute
FTC	Federal Trade Commission
GAAP	Generally Accepted Accounting Principles
GASB	Governmental Accounting Standards Board
SEC	Securities and Exchange Commission
SFAS	Statement of Financial Accounting Standard

International

ARC	Accounting Regulatory Committee
EEC	European Economic Community
EFRAG	European Financial Reporting Advisory Group
EU	European Union

IAS   International Accounting Standards
IASB   International Accounting Standards Board
IASC   International Accounting Standards Committee
IFAC   International Federation of Accountants
IFRS   International Financial Reporting Standards
IOSCO   International Organisation of Securities Commissions

Accounting terms

CCA   Current Cost Accounting
CPP   Constant Purchasing Power
EPS   Earnings per Share
HMC   Historical Money Cost
LIFO   Last In First Out
MPT   Modern Portfolio Theory
NRV   Net Realisable Value
PE   Price/Earnings (ratio or multiple)
P&L   Profit and Loss

GLOSSARY

Current Cost Accounting (CCA): system of current value accounting that continues to use money as the unit of account (unlike CPP), but shows assets and expenses at current replacement cost (normally) instead of at historical cost.

Constant Purchasing Power (CPP) accounting: method of inflation accounting that adjusts historical money costs of various dates by means of the Retail Prices Index.

Deferred tax: part of tax expense charged in accounts, not payable for some time owing to timing differences between reported and taxable profits.

Goodwill: excess of purchase price paid to acquire another company over the 'fair value' of the net separable assets acquired.

Last In First Out (LIFO): method of valuing stock which assumes for accounting purposes that the goods most *recently* purchased are sold first, even if that does not reflect physical reality.

Long-term contract: a contract that involves two or more accounting periods. Accountants have to make estimates about how much profit, if any, to recognise after part of the work has been done but before the contract is completed.

Net Realisable Value (NRV): estimated net proceeds of selling an asset (often stock), after deducting any further costs needed to complete manufacture and any related selling and distribution costs.

AUTHOR'S PREFACE

This paper has evolved from *Accountants without Standards? Compulsion or Evolution in Company Accounting* (Hobart Paper 128, October 1995). It has been updated and expanded but many aspects rely heavily on Hobart Paper 128.

The message of this Hobart Paper, even more than of Hobart 128, is that accounting – and its regulation – has taken a wrong fork in the road. Put briefly, the American, British and international standard-setters (who all agree on this direction) are now producing standards based on principles that are irrelevant for the vast majority of entities producing accounts and rejected by most professional accountants. If accounting matters, as I am convinced it does, this is a recipe for disaster.

We have far too many standards in far too much detail, and the fact that the Americans are even worse off in these respects than we are is little consolation. I conclude that all we really need is for the Companies Act to require accounts to give 'a true and fair view' of a company's performance and financial position. Anything more should be voluntary 'suggestions', not compulsory 'instructions'. Standards should relate to disclosure but not measurement, and should be for listed companies only, not for small companies and non-business entities.

What is happening in accounting is very similar to developments in the European Union – revolutionary changes whose implications most people remain oblivious to, and which have the support only of a tiny, well-meaning 'elite'. I don't believe that the 'conceptual framework' currently being used by accounting regulators can survive in anything like its present form, though so much intellectual capital has been invested in its construction and imposition that it is hard to tell when it will collapse.

Very little has been dropped from the earlier paper; but I have updated and expanded the discussion where appropriate, and tried to improve clarity throughout. The new text is nearly twice as long as Hobart Paper 128 and contains nine chapters as compared with five. A comparison of the two texts follows.

Chapter 1, 'The Purpose of Company Accounts', is the old Chapter III, with little changed.

Chapters 2 and 3, 'The Emergence of UK Accounting Standards' and 'The Emergence of International Accounting Standards' respectively, stem from the old Chapter I. Much of Chapter 3 is new.

Chapters 4 and 5, 'Arguments for Accounting Standards' and 'Arguments against Accounting Standards', match the old Chapter II.

Chapter 6, 'General Acceptance?', is new. It lists the top accountancy firms' objections to the ASB's 'Statement of Principles of Financial Reporting'.

Chapter 7, 'Political Interference', collects scattered references to this topic, especially material on inflation accounting from the old Chapter IV.

Chapter 8, 'Setting and Enforcing Standards', incorporates the rest of the old Chapter IV, with expanded discussion of cost–benefit analysis of regulation.

Chapter 9, 'Conclusions', matches the old Chapter V.

Unshackling Accountants

1 THE PURPOSE OF COMPANY ACCOUNTS

The published accounts of companies have five main purposes:

- to enable *shareholders* to monitor the performance of managers;
- to show *companies* how much profit there is to pay out in dividends to shareholders;
- to underpin *contractual arrangements*, including management bonuses;
- to help *lenders and suppliers* make decisions about providing finance;
- to provide a basis for *governments* to tax corporate profits.

No single model of accounting satisfies everyone: preparers, auditors and users may have somewhat different aims. In law, annual accounts reporting to all shareholders about corporate performance and financial position are not prospectuses inviting individuals to invest. Nor do balance sheets purport to 'value' enterprises. Probably the least imperfect approach is the orthodox stewardship model emphasising consistent disclosure and based on recoverable historical cost, prudence, matching and realised profits. It is fairly objective, it evolved gradually over many years, and it has proved able to satisfy the five main purposes of accounts for companies of all sizes.

In contrast, accounting standard-setters, who all accept the gist of the US Financial Accounting Standards Board's (FASB's) 'conceptual framework', are now attempting to impose a system based on 'decision-usefulness', prescribing measurement rules as well as disclosure. This model has developed over the past forty years and focuses on how investors in listed companies use their funds rather than on management performance. It aims to change accounts from being a report on past performance into an instrument for predicting future cash flows; and seems to suggest either that backward-looking accounts can help predict the future or that 'financial statements' themselves ought to be more forward looking.

The concept of stewardship

British and American accounting both derive from the same historical tradition and have to cope with similar pressures, though there are many differences of detail and some of principle. In both countries uncoupling the management and ownership of listed companies has made financial statements essential to enable shareholders to assess management's actions. Thus company accounts comprise an important part of regular reports to shareholders on the stewardship of directors.

For many years George O. May[1] was the senior partner of Price Waterhouse in New York. He contrasted 'those who would continue to regard financial statements as reports of progress or of stewardship, and those who would treat them as being in the

---

1   George O. May, *Financial Accounting: a Distillation of Experience*, Macmillan, London, 1943, pp. 19–21.

nature of prospectuses', adding that 'No one has a right to interpret a report of stewardship as though it were an invitation to invest.'

This argument continues today, more than sixty years later, though the Companies Act 1985 draws a clear distinction between prospectuses (Part III) and company accounts (Part VII). Companies only rarely issue a prospectus, which aims to solicit funds directly from the public; but all listed companies publish regular annual accounts. Nearly all purchases and sales of shares are between existing or new shareholders and do not directly involve the company itself.

'Stewardship' means accounting by an agent (manager) for the use of resources that the principal (owner) has supplied directly or indirectly. In 1952 the Institute of Chartered Accountants in England and Wales (ICAEW)[2] said: 'The primary purpose of the annual accounts of a business is to present information to the proprietors, showing how their funds have been utilised and the profits derived from such use.'

In 1973 the President of the Financial Executives Institute (FEI)[3] summarised the orthodox US view: 'The primary purposes of the financial statements of a business enterprise are: (1) to discharge management's obligation to report on its stewardship of the business to its stockholders, and (2) to provide the investing public with meaningful information which can be used to appraise the company's performance.'

The legal position in the UK clearly supports the stewardship

---

2   ICAEW Recommendation N15, para. 1.
3   Charles C. Hornstobel, 'Speaking Out on Financial Reporting Challenges', *Journal of Contemporary Business*, spring 1973, p. 78.

view. In 1965 counsel's opinion[4] was that 'in law the object of annual accounts is to assist shareholders in exercising control of the company by enabling them to judge how its affairs have been conducted'.

The House of Lords[5] reiterated this view in the 1990 Caparo case. Lord Jauncey observed: '… the purpose of annual accounts, so far as members are concerned, is to enable them to question the past management of the company, to exercise their voting rights … and to influence future policy and management'. And Lord Oliver said: 'I see no grounds for believing that, in enacting the statutory provisions, Parliament had in mind the provision of information for the assistance of purchasers of shares or debentures in the market.'

A 1995 draft of the Accounting Standards Board's (ASB) Statement of Principles[6] noted that: 'The objective [of financial statements] has been revised to include a specific reference to [their] use … for assessing the stewardship of management.' Those who see the main purpose of accounts as relating to stewardship must wonder at the outlook of standard-setters who treat this as an afterthought. By putting the emphasis on decision-usefulness for investors, the ASB is in effect regarding company accounts as if they were annual prospectuses.

---

4   *The Corporate Report*, a discussion paper published by the Accounting Standards Steering Committee (ASSC), London, 1975, p. 34.

5   Caparo Industries plc *v*. Dickman and others, House of Lords, 8 February 1990, Jauncey, p. 49; Oliver, p. 40, of 50-page judgment.

6   *Statement of Principles for Financial Reporting*, ASB, 1995, p. 9.

Historical cost

In recent years some accountants have enthused about various versions of current value accounting. Whatever its potential benefits this approach is far more hypothetical than most people understand and subject to wide margins of error. (The name 'current cost accounting' (CCA), coined by the 1975 Sandilands Committee in the UK, was a brilliant stroke of public relations seeming to combine 'up-to-date-ness' with reliability.) But stating assets at 'values' higher than cost could mean companies reporting profit on the basis of unrealised estimates. Such speculative accounting is extremely hazardous.

For purposes of stewardship, historical cost accounting is better than any current value system.[7] It is the only method that keeps track of an entity's resources; and it is less costly to operate and provides data that are less open to dispute. In 1962 the Jenkins Committee[8] concluded that the historical cost approach should continue to be the basis for company accounts. Even the Sandilands Committee[9] pointed out its many important advantages 'when prices are stable':

> ... historic cost accounting rests on a principle that is
> readily intelligible to the user of accounts because it is
> firmly based on the traditional common view that profit is
> the excess of revenues over historic expenditure. Centuries
> of use have also resulted in it being well established
> throughout industry and commerce and its reliance on

---

7   Yuji Ijiri, 'A Defence for Historical Cost Accounting', in Robert R. Sterling (ed.), *Asset Valuation and Income Determination*, Scholars Book Company, 1971.

8   *Report of the Company Law Committee* (Jenkins), Cmnd. 1749, HMSO, London, 1964, para. 333.

9   *Report of the Inflation Accounting Committee* (Sandilands), Cmnd. 6225, HMSO, London, September 1975, paras 271 and 273.

> normally verifiable figures of historic cost means that it
> is cheap … compared with other systems of accounting.
> … there is no doubt that overall, when prices are stable,
> historic cost accounting meets the majority of the
> requirements for information … Historically this system
> has proved to be of great value in protecting the interests of
> shareholders and creditors of companies, and, when prices
> are stable, results in a clear and unambiguous view of a
> company's affairs.

In 1988 a discussion document from the Scottish Institute[10] suggested that Net Realisable Value (NRV) might be more relevant as the basis for valuing assets in the balance sheet. It argued that historical cost accounting, though probably more objective, failed the test of additivity completely 'because pounds … of different dates … are being added together'. This charge is true of historical money cost (HMC) but not of Constant Purchasing Power (CPP) accounting, which uses the Retail Prices Index to index money costs. The ICAEW's Recommendation N15 correctly pointed out that constant purchasing power accounting 'is not strictly a proposal for a change from accounting based on historical cost'. CPP thus manages to overcome the unfitness of money as the unit of account in a period of rapid inflation while retaining all the many advantages of historical cost.

Interim accounts

The transition from accounting for 'ventures', which lasted only

---

10   ICAS (P. McMonnies, ed.), *Making Corporate Reports Valuable*, Kogan Page, London, 1988, pp. 58–9.

for a discrete period, to accounting for 'going concerns' led to the need for regular 'interim' accounts reporting on a business's financial position and performance. A 'venture' might be a ship's voyage to the Indies, with 'shareholders' who (if the ship returned) would receive their due proportion of the proceeds comprising a mixture of repayment of the original capital subscribed and a share of the profits. 'Going concerns', in contrast, required 'permanent' capital which a company would never repay to shareholders. An early English example was the formation of the New River Company[11] by Hugh Myddelton in 1609.

Thus there emerged a requirement for regular measurement of profit to determine how much a company could safely distribute to shareholders by way of periodic 'dividends' without reducing its 'capital'. Often the intention was merely to maintain the size of the business, not to increase it. Hence dividends might roughly equal profits with little or no 'retention' of profits in the business. Annual accounts, which themselves are 'interim accounts' in the context of a going concern's whole life, became the norm.

Even though the capital of a company might be permanent, individual shareholders can legally sell or transfer their shares to others. Existing shareholders (potential vendors) may naturally wish to 'value' their shares from time to time, but the company itself is less concerned to do so. Nor do balance sheets purport to value enterprises. In that respect the American expression 'net worth' for 'capital and reserves' ('shareholders' funds') is highly misleading. Balance sheets do not include all a company's assets; nor do they show all assets (or liabilities) at current value; and

---

11 See Bernard Rudden, *The New River: a legal history*, Clarendon Press, Oxford, 1985. (In 1612 King James I took a 50 per cent interest in the enterprise, which Charles I sold to Sir Hugh Myddelton in 1630.)

even if they tried to do both it makes a difference how a business *combines* discrete assets.

Some years ago the manager of the French soccer team decided not to select Eric Cantona, then widely regarded as the best footballer in the world. The reason was that Cantona did not fit in with other members of the side, so the value of a team including him might have been less than the sum of all its players. (A reverse sporting example might be Mike Brearley. On technical playing merit his claim to a place in the England cricket team was marginal, yet many people felt he was worth it for his captaincy alone.) A business, of course, should normally be worth *more* than the sum of the realisable values of its net assets, otherwise it would pay to sell them all.

In the context of stewardship reporting, publishing interim accounts more frequently than once a year may be of little value. There was plenty of dissent from a proposed EU rule (now dropped) requiring quarterly accounts for listed companies. Was this just a misguided attempt to match the Securities and Exchange Commission (SEC), which has required quarterly reports in the USA since 1970? Certainly the shorter the period of the profit and loss account the larger the percentage margin of error in reported profits.[12]

The ASB published a non-mandatory statement in 1997 on interim reports (meaning reports covering periods of less than a year). The chairman of the Financial Reporting Council (FRC) asserted that: 'such [interim] reports, together with other informa-

---

12 Also, the shorter the reporting period, the greater the advantage of accrual accounting over cash flows in reflecting performance. Patricia M. Dechow, 'Accounting earnings and cash flows as measures of firm performance', *Journal of Accounting and Economics*, 18, 1994, pp. 3–42.

tion … available throughout the year, are a necessary input to the making of informed investment decisions'. But there was no discussion of the desirable frequency of so-called 'interim' reports. If quarterly accounts, why not weekly? Does one really need always to be absolutely 'up to date'? In James Hilton's novel *Lost Horizon*,[13] the hero remarked that time meant less to the lamas in their mountain retreat than it does to most people in the everyday world. 'If I were in London I wouldn't always be eager to see the latest hour-old newspaper and you at Shangri-La are no more eager to see a year-old one.'

A better interim measure of business performance might be regular quarterly dividends, along US lines, in place of the normal UK practice of irregular 'interim' and 'final' dividends. This would both clarify and make more frequent the explicit 'signal' from management to shareholders; which being in cash would be hard to overlook and easy to understand. But it need not involve external reporting of *profits* over very short periods, since companies may legally pay dividends out of past cumulative retained profits without necessarily requiring current profits to cover them.

Given the highly artificial nature of one-year accounting periods, it is perhaps surprising that there has not been more interest in experimenting with longer accounting periods – say of five or ten years.[14] (Auditing firms might of course be reluctant to lose regular annual repeat business.) Accounting for such longer

---

13 James Hilton, *Lost Horizon*, Macmillan, London, 1933, ch. 6.

14 See, for example: (a) May, op. cit., p. 45; (b) D. R. Myddelton, 'Consolidated Nationalised Industry Accounts 1948–1970: Published Figures Adjusted for Currency Debasement', *Accounting and Business Research*, spring 1972 (examples of ten-year accounts); (c) D. R. Myddelton, '25 years of Currency Debasement and the Accounts of Lucas Industries', in Tony Grundy and Keith Ward (eds), *Strategic Business Finance*, Kogan Page, 1996 (examples of five-year accounts).

periods can mitigate some of the inevitable margins of error of one-year accounts which standard-setters tend to downplay. For instance,[15] why not try a three-year or five-year moving average for operating statements? Certainly it might make sense to calculate volatile earnings per share not just year by year but also using three-year or five-year averages. Or what about restating financial reports in subsequent years?[16] 'As future events evolve and uncertainty is resolved, our understanding of the *past* is increasingly improved.'

'Decision-usefulness'

In 1966 the American Accounting Association[17] (of academics) (AAA) proposed a switch away from stewardship reporting and towards using accounting for economic decision-making ('decision-usefulness'). Soon afterwards the Trueblood Committee[18] suggested that financial statements should help investors to predict, compare and evaluate potential cash flows to them in terms of amount, timing and related uncertainty. This led on to the assertion in the first part of the 'Conceptual Framework'[19] of the US Financial Accounting Standards Board (FASB): 'Financial reporting should provide information that is useful to

---

15   David F. Linowes, in Robert R. Sterling (ed.), *Institutional Issues in Public Accounting*, Scholars Book Co., 1974, p. 402.

16   Baruch Lev and Paul Zarowin, 'The Boundaries of Financial Reporting and How to Extend Them', *Journal of Accounting Research*, 37(2), autumn 1999, pp. 353–85.

17   American Accounting Association (AAA), *A Statement of Basic Accounting Theory*, 1966.

18   AICPA, *Report of the [Trueblood] Study Group on the Objectives of Financial Statements*, 1973.

19   FASB, *Objectives of Financial Reporting by Business Enterprises*, 1978.

present and potential investors and creditors and other users in making rational investment, credit and similar decisions.'

The FASB's ambitious Conceptual Framework project absorbed huge amounts of time and money in the 1970s before ending in 1985. The International Accounting Standards Committee's (IASC's) 1989 'Framework' and (ten years later) the UK ASB's 1999 'Statement of Principles' more or less followed its conclusions. The impetus behind the idea was a school of academics seeking a comprehensive, self-consistent, 'scientific' deductive system of accounting. In contrast most professional accountants favoured the eclectic, judgemental, pragmatic tradition in which some practices may conflict with others. 'Not a statement of eternal truth but a list of temporary working hypotheses.'[20]

Solomons[21] thought a US-type conceptual framework could also help defend UK accounting from government interference; though constructing it, like standard setting, is itself a political process.[22] He assumed that regulators could know what best accounting is and wanted their views imposed on everyone. But there is no agreement today on what *is* 'best', and even if there were it might not last long.

Most comment on the Conceptual Framework project has been critical. One expert[23] said: 'There are only a few fundamental issues in financial accounting. The FASB ducked them all.' Another[24]

20 M. J. Mumford, *British Accounting Review*, 21(4), December 1989, p. 382.

21 David Solomons, 'The Political Implications of Accounting and Accounting Standard Setting', *Accounting and Business Research*, spring 1983.

22 Pelham Gore, *The FASB Conceptual Framework Project 1973–1985*, Manchester University Press, 1992.

23 R. N. Anthony, 'We don't have the accounting concepts we need', *Harvard Business Review*, Jan./Feb. 1987, p. 75.

24 Gore, op. cit., p. 1.

remarked: 'Superlatives have been applied to its inputs, but not to its outputs.' Similar efforts in other countries appear to have had no more success. Indeed, not everyone would regard 'success' in this regard as worth having.

Other 'conceptual framework' discussions[25] have also suggested 'decision-usefulness' as the main purpose of financial reporting. But the studies themselves[26] usually cite no empirical evidence either about decisions or about users. One critic[27] said the FASB adopted a normative, deductive, decision-usefulness approach without properly considering alternatives. He pointed out that the (US) Governmental Accounting Standards Board (GASB) based its objectives document not on decision-usefulness but on accountability and stewardship.

As Bromwich[28] noted, the FASB's hierarchy of qualities 'all flow from the overriding objective of providing accounting information useful for decisions. They therefore suffer from our lack of understanding of the models used for decision making'. In other words the FASB doesn't know what it is talking about! Like the ASB and the IASC it just *assumes* the basis for its accounting standards.

The three British academics who later became members of the UK Accounting Standards Board all liked the decision-usefulness approach. (Two of them went on to lead the International

25 In particular, ASSC, *The Corporate Report*, 1975; ICAS, *Making Corporate Reports Valuable*, 1988; ICAEW, *Framework for the Preparation and Presentation of Financial Statements*, 1989 (Solomons); IASC, *Framework*, 1989.

26 Michael J. Mumford, 'Users, characteristics and standards', in M. J. Mumford and K. V. Peasnell (eds), *Philosophical Perspectives on Accounting*, Routledge, London, 1993.

27 Gore, op. cit., p. 61.

28 Michael Bromwich, *Financial Reporting, Information and Capital Markets*, Pitman Publishing, London, 1992, p. 287.

Accounting Standards body.) Carsberg, who had advised the American FASB, admitted[29] that its conceptual framework's findings were mostly assertions with no supporting evidence. Tweedie and Whittington[30] accepted the broad consensus on the purpose of financial reports which all these documents (listed in note 25) share.

Most of these conceptual framework efforts outline what people think company accounts *ought* to be aiming at; '... decision-usefulness fails to characterise accounting as it is, only how it might be'.[31] In focusing on decision-usefulness rather than stewardship their authors seem to be deliberately trying to get away from what most people think company accounts are actually meant to achieve.

In 1976 the FASB carried out a survey to determine how many people agreed with the Trueblood objectives. Apparently[32] it surprised the Board to learn that only 37 per cent of the respondents believed that providing information useful for making economic decisions was an objective of financial accounting. Similar criticisms of Accounting Research Studies 1 and 3 of the American Institute of Certified Public Accountants (AICPA) in the early 1960s halted further work on them. Hence there is a growing danger of an 'expectations gap' in accounting.

---

29 Bryan Carsberg, 'The US Conceptual Framework for Financial Reporting' (lecture given in Cardiff, February 1982), in *Contemporary Issues in Accounting*, Pitman Publishing, Bath, 1984, p. 106.

30 David Tweedie and Geoffrey Whittington, 'Financial Reporting: Current Problems and their Implications for Systematic Reform', *Accounting and Business Research*, 81, winter 1990.

31 Michael Page, 'The ASB's Proposed Objective of Financial Statements: Marching in Step Backwards? A Review Essay', *British Accounting Review*, 24(1), March 1992, p. 79.

32 Nicholas Dopuch and Shyam Sunder, 'FASB's Statement on Objectives and Elements of Financial Accounting: A Review', *Accounting Review*, January 1980, pp. 1–21.

It has been claimed[33] that 'preparers [of accounts] have had considerable success in limiting the influence of decision-usefulness theory on practice'. Textbook writers 'devote one section to a summary of the conceptual framework ... and then forget about it in all of the other chapters. GAAP [Generally Accepted Accounting Principles] is the bible that textbook writers choose to interpret and teach. Their acceptance of decision-usefulness theory is comparable to the adherent to a religion that shows up in a house of worship twice a year.'

The accounts of non-business bodies can hardly be useful to investors in making decisions. So the 'decision-usefulness' school has to argue that the purpose of accounting differs as between business and non-business entities. Others may prefer Anthony's view[34] that the primary focus of accounting in both kinds of organisation is on measuring net income (profit) to report the extent of success in maintaining financial capital. Therefore accounting practices should be broadly the same and stewardship reporting can remain the primary purpose of accounts both for business and for non-business entities. Indeed, SFAS 117 on the financial statements of not-for-profit organisations[35] states that 'external financial reporting should focus on the interests of present and potential resource providers'. They want to know about 'organization performance and ... management stewardship'. The Company Law Review

---

33 George Staubus, *The Decision-Usefulness Theory of Accounting: a limited history*, Garland Publishing, New York, 2000, p. 338.

34 Robert N. Anthony, *Should Business and Non-business Accounting Be Different?*, Harvard Business School Press, Cambridge, MA, 1989.

35 Statement of Financial Accounting Standard (SFAS) 117, *Financial Statements of Not-for-Profit Organizations*, 1993, para. 43.

Committee also rejected the decision-usefulness view.[36]

In the UK the Companies Act requires company accounts to provide financial information to its existing shareholders *as a class*. Apart from possibly voting to reduce a proposed dividend (which hardly ever happens in practice) the only 'investment' decisions open to the shareholders as a class are whether or not to wind up the company and whether or not to accept a takeover bid. Few people would argue that it is a primary purpose of 'going concern' annual company accounts to assist with the former decision, and it seems doubtful whether they can help much with the latter.

After a wide-ranging discussion, Benston[37] concluded that the evidence does not suggest that published annual financial statements are useful for investment decisions. They might, however, confirm what investors had learned from other sources.[38] This should be no surprise: company accounts report on what has happened in the past whereas people making economic decisions care more about the *future*. A recent study[39] found that both analysts and fund managers thought a company's annual report and accounts significantly less useful than personal contact with the company. Agency theory clearly implies that

36 Andrew Higson, *Corporate Financial Reporting*, Sage Publications, 2003, p. xi.

37 George J. Benston, 'The Effectiveness and Effects of the SEC's Accounting Disclosure Requirements', in Henry Manne (ed.), *Economic Policy and the Regulation of Corporate Securities*, American Institute for Public Policy Research, Washington, DC, 1969, p. 140.

38 See K. V. Peasnell, *The Usefulness of Accounting Information to Investors*, ICRA, Lancaster, 1973.

39 Richard G. Barker, 'The market for information – evidence from finance directors, analysts and fund managers', *Accounting and Business Research*, 29(1), winter 1998. Both analysts and fund managers gave a median ranking of 3 (on a 5-point scale) to the importance of the report and accounts.

stewardship reporting mainly affects the behaviour not of *owners* but of managers.[40]

Predicting future results

According to the FASB's Conceptual Framework, past accounting earnings provide a better basis than past cash flows for predicting an enterprise's future cash flows. But if predicting future cash flows is the primary purpose of accounts, this suggests that the more companies smooth earnings the better. Some accounting standards, such as deferred tax and the percentage completion method for long-term contracts, do have precisely such an effect, though Financial Reporting Standard (FRS) 3 points strongly in the opposite direction.

In the 1931 Royal Mail Steamship case[41] the company had drawn on secret taxation reserves to convert an 'actual' loss into a reported profit. Lord Kylsant (chairman) and Mr Moreland (auditor) were both acquitted on the charge of wilfully deceiving the shareholders. This was probably due to evidence of widespread similar accounting practices at that time. But practice in this respect changed long before there were formal accounting standards in the UK.

The Sandilands Committee distinguished between 'operating gains' (the excess of current sales revenue over 'current costs') and 'holding gains' (increases in assets' current replacement costs). Sandilands claimed that for most companies the annual operating

---

40   Page, op. cit.

41   Sir Patrick Hastings, 'The Case of the Royal Mail', reprinted in W. T. Baxter and Sidney Davidson (eds), *Studies in Accounting Theory*, Sweet & Maxwell, London, 2nd edn, 1962.

gains 'may well provide a useful guide' to the company's long-run future earnings.[42] The report did not further justify this amazing assertion. (Does it also apply to operating *losses*?) Business profits depend on the success of speculation about an *uncertain* future. Edwards and Bell, who made a similar statement,[43] recognised it was 'rather unrealistic' to assume that production processes will not change.

In 1847 the directors of the Peninsular and Orient Company argued that:

'Proprietors at a distance forming their opinion of the future position of the company from published accounts of past transactions could scarcely avoid arriving at erroneous conclusions.'[44]

There was, of course, much less disclosure in company accounts 150 years ago than there is today. (Indeed, the company used the passage quoted to justify not publishing accounts at all!) But it still seems unlikely in theory and unproven in practice that accounts reporting on past performance and financial position can help much in forecasting an enterprise's future cash flows.

The ASB's 1995 Statement of Principles exposure draft[45] stated: 'Information about financial position and past performance is frequently used in making predictions of future financial position and performance.' That may well be so. The fact that many people like to consult horoscopes hardly proves their usefulness in making predictions.

---

42 Sandilands, op. cit., para. 168.
43 Edgar O. Edwards and Philip W. Bell, *The Theory and Measurement of Business Income*, University of California Press, Berkeley, 1961, p. 99.
44 Quoted in Guy Naylor, *Company Law for Shareholders*, Hobart Paper 7, IEA, London, 1960, p. 12.
45 ASB, *Statement of Principles for Financial Reporting*, exposure draft, 1995, para. 2-11.

In his *General Theory*, Keynes[46] referred to the convention 'that the existing state of affairs will continue indefinitely except in so far as we have specific reasons to expect a change'. But he at once went on to point out: 'This does not mean that we really believe that the existing state of affairs will continue indefinitely. We know from extensive experience that this is most unlikely.'

But the ASB went further: 'Information about the economic resources controlled by the enterprise and the use made of them in the past is useful in predicting the enterprise's ability to generate cash from them in the future.'[47] It would be fascinating to know the basis for this bold assertion, which remained (in slightly different words) in the 1999 Statement of Principles.

As Beaver[48] explained, if a market is efficient, 'no amount of security analysis, based on published financial statement data, will lead to abnormal returns [for an investor] … The FASB should actively discourage investors' beliefs that accounting data can be used to detect overvalued or undervalued securities'.

Most studies[49] conclude that annual earnings appear to follow a random path, hence that past earnings growth does not help predict future growth. This result has been called 'one of the most robust empirical findings in the financial statement literature'.[50] In any case, it is cash flows for many years ahead which affect the

---

46 J.M. Keynes, *The General Theory of Employment, Interest and Money*, Macmillan, London, 1936, p. 152.

47 ASB, op. cit., para. 1-10. A similar statement appears in the 1999 revised exposure draft, para. 1-16(a), and in the final 1999 Statement of Principles, para. 1-14(a).

48 William H. Beaver, 'What Should be the FASB's Objectives?', *Journal of Account-ancy*, August 1973.

49 See R. Watts and R. Leftwich, 'The Time Series of Accrual Accounting Earnings', *Journal of Accounting Research*, autumn 1977.

50 G. Foster, *Financial Statement Analysis*, Prentice-Hall, Englewood Cliffs, NJ, 1986, 2nd edn, p. 240.

value of shares, not just next year's. A recent study[51] found 'the accuracy of analysts' long-term forecasts is extremely low'. The fact is that fundamental analysis of accounting reports is not very 'useful' to investors in predicting future profits. Nor is technical analysis of past share price movements useful in predicting future share prices. That is why most unit trust advertisements carry the warning: 'Past performance is no guide to the future'.

Disagreement about the purpose of company accounts can affect what kind of regulation might be suitable. Chapters 2 and 3 describe the emergence of accounting standards in the UK and elsewhere; and Chapters 4 and 5 set out the arguments for and against standards.

---

51   Richard D. F. Harris, *Journal of Business Finance and Accounting*, June/July 1999, pp. 725–55.

2 THE EMERGENCE OF UK ACCOUNTING STANDARDS

From early in Queen Victoria's reign UK governments used Companies Acts to regulate company accounts. The last 150 years can be split into four periods:

1856–1900 Neither accounts nor audit generally required.

1900–48 Audit required of balance sheet only.

1948–90 Audit required of group balance sheet and profit and loss account, showing 'a true and fair view'. Detailed voluntary 'recommendations' by professional accounting bodies about measurement and disclosure; then 'Statements of Standard Accounting Practice' (SSAPs), which everyone was 'expected' to follow.

1990–2004 Compulsory Financial Reporting Standards (FRSs) mostly based on new conceptual framework.

A true and fair view

For more than half a century British law has required accounts to give 'a true and fair view' of the state of a company's affairs and of its profit or loss for the financial year. This rule now applies across the whole European Union. According to Hopwood[1] this emphas-

---

1   Anthony G. Hopwood, 'Ambiguity, Knowledge and Territorial Claims', *British Accounting Review*, 22(1), March 1990, p. 85.

ises the need for discretionary self-regulation rather than statutory standards.

We should note that *more than one* true and fair view may be possible at one time:[2] the word 'a' is important. Thus we can sometimes say 'A is right, but B is not wrong either'.[3] For example, in the UK declining-balance depreciation is much less common than straight-line depreciation, yet everyone regards it as a perfectly valid method of accounting. Two otherwise identical companies could report different profits (and assets) because they chose, quite properly, to write different amounts off fixed assets. Similar companies might also make different provisions for bad debts or for writing down damaged stock below original cost. To such accounting choices involving professional judgement there can never be a precisely 'correct' solution.

The law[4] now requires companies to say whether their accounts follow accounting standards and if not to give details with reasons. The legal requirement for company (or group) accounts to give a true and fair view is overriding.[5] Hence there may be a need either to provide *more* information if merely following all the detailed rules would not suffice, or even to *depart* from specific rules if complying with them would be incompatible with giving a true and fair view. As West[6] points out, 'Compliance with rules per se

---

2   Ken Sharp, head of the Government Accounting Service, in a very rare case in which the courts did have to decide about 'a true and fair view'. R. K. Ashton, 'The Argyll Foods case: a legal analysis', *Accounting and Business Research*, 65, winter 1986, p. 4.

3   Gilbert Byrne, 'To What Extent Can the Practice of Accounting be Reduced to Rules and Standards?', *Journal of Accountancy*, November 1937, pp. 364–79.

4   Companies Act 1985, Section 36A.

5   Ibid., Sections 228 and 230.

6   Brian P. West, *Professionalism and Accounting Rules*, Routledge, London, 2003, pp. 1, 197.

is not what determines the reliability and usefulness of accounting information. … The legislative provision of "true and fair" specifies an overall quality standard for company accounts. It is an *output* standard. However the accounting rules … are input standards … '

A true and fair view used to imply 'consistent application of generally accepted accounting principles'[7] involving the appropriate measurement, classification and disclosure of items. More recently Arden[8] has suggested it means little more than compliance with official accounting standards. She believes that courts are likely so to find even if a standard were to require a treatment that is neither generally accepted nor prevails in practice. Her opinion, which has still not been directly tested in the courts, downplays the need for integrity and independent judgement ('not qualities which can be insured by regulation'[9]).

There have been hardly any judicial rulings in the past fifty years to reveal what the courts think the phrase 'a true and fair view' means. Does this imply the phrase is so well understood that disputed cases simply do not arise? More likely it means that nobody knows precisely what it now means, in which case all professional accountants are free to *make up their own mind* about this overriding legal requirement.

---

7   Institute of Chartered Accountants in England and Wales (ICAEW), Recommendation N18, 1958.

8   Mary Arden, 'Accounting Standards Board: The True and Fair Requirement', Appendix to *Foreword to Accounting Standards*, ASB, London, 1993.

9   George O. May, 'Improvement in Financial Accounts', *Journal of Accountancy*, May 1937.

Company law

Various Companies Acts dating back more than 150 years have set out legal requirements to do with accounts (as well as many other matters). In effect these are government-imposed 'accounting standards'. Until recently they dealt almost entirely with disclosure, not with measurement.

The 1845 Act required companies to publish audited balance sheets. Apparently[10] the 1856 Act was originally intended to increase the degree of regulation, but Parliament reflected a national attitude of laissez-faire by *withdrawing* the need both for audit and for publication. The 1855 Act had introduced limited liability, a key change affecting both creditors and shareholders.

The 1900 Act reinstated the need for audit and required balance sheets to give 'a true and correct view'. From today's perspective it seems astonishing that at the height of Britain's worldwide commercial influence, 'between 1856 and 1900 … company reporting and auditing [was] conducted on a purely voluntary basis'.[11] This implies that company accounts may now be somewhat *over*-regulated.

Over the past hundred years wide-ranging reviews at regular intervals have preceded most major changes to UK company law. After the Loreburn Report (1906) the 1907 Act required 'public' companies to file balance sheets (the 1905 Reid Report having proposed that *all* companies did so). As a result of the Greene Report (1926) the 1929 Act required companies to publish profit

---

10   Christopher Napier, 'The History of Financial Reporting in the United Kingdom', in Peter Walton (ed.), *European Financial Reporting: A History*, Academic Press, 1995, p. 265.

11   T. A. Lee and R. H. Parker, *The Evolution of Corporate Financial Reporting*, Thomas Nelson, 1979, p. 18.

and loss accounts as well (though the 1918 Wrensbury Report had taken a contrary view).

Following the Cohen Report (1945), the 1948 Act required group accounts for the first time, made profit and loss accounts subject to audit and changed the requirement for 'a true and correct view' to 'a true and fair view'. More than half a century later two aspects of the 1948 Act are striking. The first is the relative brevity of its accounting and audit requirements, only 26 pages in total (there were a mere twelve pages in the 1929 Act). The second noteworthy point is how frequently the Act allowed sensible exceptions to its provisions, sometimes subject to approval by the Board of Trade (now the Department of Trade and Industry (DTI)).

The Jenkins Report (1962) led to the 1967 Act with further disclosure requirements on sales (turnover) and changes in fixed assets. Before then UK company accounts rarely disclosed annual turnover; in fact Benston[12] concluded that a 1934 government requirement in the USA for companies to disclose sales did not provide investors with anything useful. In the early 1960s a number of UK companies even *ceased* to publish turnover figures[13] on the grounds that people might misinterpret them.

The EEC Fourth Directive on Company Law brought two important changes for the UK. The 1981 Act imposed *measurement* rules for the first time, including four general accounting principles which SSAP 2 had set out in 1972: going concern, consistency, prudence and accruals. In addition to other new disclosure require-

---

12   George J. Benston, *Regulating Financial Markets*, Hobart Paper 135, IEA, London, 1998, p. 77.

13   Harold Rose, *Disclosure in Company Accounts*, Eaton Paper 1, IEA, London, 2nd edn, 1965, p. 19.

ments it also prescribed for the first time in the UK a number of approved *formats* for balance sheets and profit and loss accounts which differed in several respects from previous practice.

The 1985 Act consolidated five earlier Acts. The 1989 Act amending it gave effect to the EEC Seventh Directive dealing with group accounts. The amended 1985 Act, which is still in force today, contains no fewer than 187 pages on accounts and audit, more than *seven times* as many as the 1948 Act.

A new Companies Act is currently in the legislative pipeline. After the first major UK review of company law for many years the Company Law Review Steering Group's Final Report in June 2001 proposed a number of radical changes. In July 2003, however, came news of further delay, so it is not clear when (or whether) its substance will become law.

This is a 'cost' of regulation which is often overlooked: failure to revise damaging or out-of-date legislation. It is a sobering thought that large parts of most new statutes are merely trying to overcome problems that earlier ones have caused. There is a dilemma here. Insisting on due process may mean that changing the rules can take a long time. But allowing regulators too much discretion risks them simply ignoring everyone else's views. One answer might be a 'sunset' clause requiring regular re-endorsement, perhaps every fifteen years or so, otherwise an accounting standard would lapse.

Recommendations, 1945–69

From 1945 to 1969 the ICAEW produced for its members a series of Recommendations on Accounting Principles. These were voluntary guidelines on best practice which sometimes allowed for several alternative approaches. The topics included: tax, inflation, group accounts, valuing stock and the format of accounts.

In 1969 the ICAEW also began to publish *Financial Reporting: a survey of UK published accounts*. This annual series showed the extent of various practices (often by sampling 300 companies of various sizes) and the monthly *Company Reporting* has fulfilled a similar function since 1990. Both have been useful in showing which accounting treatments are common ('generally accepted') and in discussing problems.

Towards the end of this period discontent with the accounting profession flared up when in October 1967 the General Electric Company (GEC) made a takeover bid for Associated Electrical Industries (AEI). As part of its response AEI forecast a pre-tax profit of £10 million for the calendar year. After GEC won control the final AEI 1967 accounts disclosed a £4.5 million *loss*, a 'difference' of nearly £15 million (about £170 million in today's money). A subsequent inquiry ascribed about one third of the difference to matters of *fact* and two-thirds to matters of *judgement*, mainly about the likely outcome of certain long-term contracts.

The accounting aspects of the GEC/AEI takeover were really a storm in a teacup. In 1967 AEI group sales were £260 million a year and stocks and work-in-progress about £100 million. So the entire 'difference' represented 15 per cent of stocks and just over 5 per cent of annual sales, which is hardly outside a normal margin of error. And the problems behind the AEI profit forecasts still exist today. According to one writer: 'At the ICAEW conference at Cambridge in June 1979, we considered the "spectacular mistakes" of the sixties which were among the influences leading to the introduction of accounting standards. The general opinion was that the problems of AEI-GEC, Pergamon, Vehicle and General, and so on, would not have been prevented by our existing accounting standards.'[14]

DTI inspectors in the early 1990s looking into the affairs of Atlantic Computers plc[15] came to a similar conclusion. They did not believe that the absence of an accounting standard dealing with lease broking was a major cause of the defects in the company's accounts between 1981 and 1988.

The Accounting Standards Committee, 1970–90

The ICAEW felt it had to respond to the GEC/AEI 'scandal'. Otherwise it was afraid that the government would interfere, which everyone agreed would be the worst possible outcome. As a result, in December 1969 the ICAEW published a Statement of Intent 'to advance accounting standards' by:

- publishing authoritative statements on best accounting practice;
- exposing draft accounting standards more widely;
- recommending disclosure of accounting bases when accounts include significant items which depend on judgement or estimates;
- recommending disclosure of departures from accounting standards.

---

14 P. J. Custis, 'Reporting Corporate Performance – For What Purpose?' (Deloitte Lecture at Birmingham, October 1979), in *Contemporary Issues in Accounting*, Pitman Publishing, Bath, May 1984, p. 21.

15 *Report of DTI Inspectors on Atlantic Computers plc*, DTI, London, July 1994, para. 5.109.

At first the Accounting Standards Steering Committee was a committee of the ICAEW alone. (The word 'Steering' was dropped after half a dozen years.) But the Scottish Institute was reluctant to be left out. Until then it had chosen *not* to issue guidelines to its own members, on the grounds that they might discourage future progress and embarrass (or even insult) members who disagreed with them. So in the end the ASC contained twenty part-time unpaid delegates from all the main professional accounting bodies, each of which had to approve every standard.

Failure to comply with the ASC's Statements of Standard Accounting Practice might cause the auditors to 'qualify' their report. Members of the profession were expected to observe standards or to disclose and explain departures from them. Accounting standards were not a comprehensive code of rigid rules. In judging exceptional or borderline cases it would be important to have regard to the spirit of accounting standards and to bear in mind the overriding requirement to give a true and fair view.

There is an important contrast here between accounting and taxation. Tax is based on law, so that tax avoidance is legal and tax evasion is illegal. (The notion of some legal tax avoidance infringing the 'spirit' of the tax laws, which Lord Goff seemed to suggest in the 1991 Ensign Tankers case, is nonsense.) But there is an overriding need in accounting to give 'a true and fair view': the requirement is itself part of the law. So the 'spirit' of the accounting rules certainly does matter; indeed, it dominates, even if nobody can define exactly what 'a true and fair view' means.

The ASC issued eighteen standards in its first decade, seven in its second, and revised several standards at least once. Ten are still outstanding (see Appendix 1). The later standards tended to deal with difficult topics more to do with measurement than disclosure, such as foreign currency translation, finance leases and pensions.

The Accounting Standards Committee earned the following warm tribute: 'In retrospect, its achievements were considerable, given [its] modest resources, and although some of its standards can be criticised, collectively they improved UK GAAP beyond recognition from the state of financial reporting practice at the time of its creation in 1970.'[16]

Post hoc ergo propter hoc. The quality of UK accounting would almost certainly have improved even in the absence of accounting standards, as it had done in the previous twenty years. The proper contrast is not with the starting point in 1970 but with what the 1990 position would have been without the ASC, which we can only guess. In the twenty years since 1970 there were indeed some improvements: in valuing stocks, the treatment of finance leases and disclosure of accounting policies. But there were some disasters too: in inflation accounting, deferred tax and accounting for goodwill.

During most of the ASC's life the problem of accounting for inflation was on the agenda. The pound lost no less than 85 per cent of its purchasing power between 1970 and 1990, a debasement of the British currency quite unprecedented in sterling's thousand-year history. On this topic the ASC clearly failed, though government interference made things worse (see Chapter 7). People generally lost confidence in the ASC, and there was also concern about its 'lack of teeth' to enforce its standards.

As a result the Dearing Committee[17] was set up in 1987 to review

16   Allister Wilson, Mike Davies, Matthew Curtis and Greg Wilkinson-Riddle, *UK & International GAAP*, Butterworths Tolley for Ernst & Young, London, 7th edn, 2001, p. 8.

17   ICAEW, *The Making of Accounting Standards* (Report of the Review Committee under the Chairmanship of Sir Ron Dearing), September 1988, pp. 7, 18.

the standard-setting process. Its report acknowledged the existence of 'a small body of opinion' holding that standards 'inhibit preparers and auditors of accounts from applying their expert judgement ... and that, on balance, standards hinder rather than help the development of fair financial reporting': that is my own view.

But the committee concluded that 'the balance of argument tells strongly in favour of the 1970 decision to develop accounting standards.' The main factors were 'the complexity of the decisions faced by the preparers and auditors of accounts, and the pressures to which they can be exposed; ... the need to avoid ambiguity; and ... the value ... of having information prepared on a consistent, fair and reasonably comparable basis'.

Dearing stated: 'The purpose of accounting standards is to provide authoritative *but not mandatory* guidance on the interpretation of what constitutes a true and fair view' (emphasis added). This seems very similar to the aim of the ICAEW's Recommendations. The report went on: 'Our recommendations are concerned with increasing [*sic*] the quality and timeliness of accounting standards, reducing the permitted options, and promoting compliance with them.' They led to the formation of the Financial Reporting Council and the Accounting Standards Board.

The Accounting Standards Board, 1990 to the present

Enter the [Financial] Accounting Standards Board. What is needed, so the story goes, is a group which will not knuckle under to the vested interests of client groups, which will not 'fiddle while Rome burns' and one which will act decisively to restore to its once glorious heights the public's faith in financial reporting. A new group, untarnished by the problems of the past and better constituted to overcome its predecessor's shortcomings can give the public what it expects. Or can it?

The above paragraph was actually written[18] in 1973 about the FASB in the United States. But it also fits the UK scene in 1990, when the ASB replaced the ASC.

The Accounting Standards Board differed from its forerunner, the Accounting Standards Committee, in several respects. Two of the ASB's members are full-time: the chairman and a technical director. They and the other eight members are appointed by a Financial Reporting Council (FRC) comprising some 25 representatives of various parties concerned with company accounts – preparers, auditors, users – not just members of the accounting profession. Despite Dearing's statement of purpose, Financial Reporting Standards under the new system are in effect mandatory.

The new regime's enforcement body, the Financial Reporting Review Panel (FRRP), aims to ensure that companies produce accounts of adequate quality, not to punish offenders, though company directors may be personally liable for costs, which seems outrageous. (To level the playing field perhaps FRRP members should also be potentially liable in this way?) Each year the Review Panel pursues about thirty out of the forty or so cases drawn to its attention, but in future it proposes to initiate some reviews itself instead of just reacting to complaints. Less than a quarter of its cases have required corrective action, usually to do with disclo-

---

18   John Shank, 'The Pursuit of Accounting Standards – Whither and Whence', *Journal of Contemporary Business*, spring 1973, p. 86.

sure rather than measurement, which often means amending the accounting treatment in subsequent years. The Review Panel's own prestige would suffer if a court were to reject its views, hence (it has been suggested[19]) when it threatens to take companies to court there may sometimes be an element of bluff. But companies may be 'even more anxious to avoid legal action because they have so little to gain'.[20]

Following the US example there is also an Urgent Issues Task Force (UITF) to deal quickly with important emerging problems. It is supposed to apply relevant accounting standards or company law where there are conflicting or unsatisfactory interpretations. So far it has published 38 'abstracts', many of which have been subsumed in subsequent standards. The ASB may have up to three dissenters (out of ten members) in issuing an accounting standard, but the UITF may have no more than two out of a maximum voting membership of sixteen with respect to its 'abstracts'. These are 'not-quite standards'.

Statements of Recommended Practice (SORPs) are also not-quite standards. They supplement (but cannot override) accounting standards and legal and other requirements in the light of the special factors prevailing in a particular industry or sector. For the purpose of issuing SORPs the ASB recognises industry or sectoral bodies, which have to follow an ASB code of practice. FRS 18 on Accounting Policies requires entities to say if their accounts fall within a SORP's scope, whether they comply with its provisions, and if not why not.

---

19 Doreen McBarnet and Christopher Whelan, *Creative Accounting and the Cross-eyed Javelin Thrower*, John Wiley & Sons, Chichester, 1999, pp. 82–96.
20 Tony Hines et al., 'We're off to see the Wizard', *Accounting, Auditing and Accountability Journal*, 14(1), 2001, p. 78.

The ASB issued twenty Financial Reporting Standards in its first ten years (see Appendix 1). Several of them related more to disclosure than to measurement. The Board had to steer a tricky course between appearing weak and risking offence to auditors or finance directors. Its first chairman, Sir David Tweedie (now chairman of the International Accounting Standards Board), was quite ready to argue publicly for the ASB's views. Maybe no other group could have done the job better. No doubt the Board's members were smart and well meaning, though they are not the only accountants meriting this description. But the question remains whether any group of people should tell professional accountants in great detail how to do their job.

The ASB has proliferated discussion papers, exposure drafts, financial reporting standards, UITF proposals, etc. The ten remaining standards (SSAPs) from the ASC average twelve and a half pages each, including notes and examples. But the first twenty FRSs from the ASB average eighty pages each (see also Appendix 1), over *six times* as long. The explanation section, which is often extensive, is normally to be 'regarded as part of the statement of standard accounting practice insofar as it assists in interpreting the statement'. The result is that (excluding the Companies Act) UK accounting standards in issue currently total more than 1,800 pages.

'Accounting standards' sometimes duplicate and sometimes contradict company law. Many of the specific disclosure requirements in company law either overlap with others or call for pointless detail. There is scope for a very substantial reduction.[21]

---

21 See, for example, Ernst & Young's *Views on Disclosure in Company Accounts* (December 1992), which makes fifty specific suggestions: ten for simplification, 25 for deleting company law requirements on disclosure, and fifteen for deleting SSAP or FRS requirements.

Appendix 3 details eight examples where UK accounting standards appear to conflict with Schedule 4 of the Companies Act 1985. There may be others.

The ASB's most important work so far has been developing its Statement of Principles, which was published in 1999 (after several drafts over a number of years). This document is similar to the Conceptual Frameworks of the US Financial Accounting Standards Board and the International Accounting Standards Committee. The Statement of Principles aims to transform orthodox accounting by diluting the principles of historical cost, prudence, realisation and matching (see Chapter 6).

What accounting standards cover

Accounting standards, together with the legal rules in the Companies Act, cover five kinds of requirements: scope, definition, presentation, disclosure and measurement.

(i) *Scope* means the kind of entity or industry or transaction to which standards apply. Some standards exclude certain kinds of *entity*, others certain *industries*, and others certain kinds of *transaction*. The ASB says[22] its Principles are intended to be relevant to financial reporting by profit-oriented entities regardless of size and, broadly speaking, also by not-for-profit entities. The Companies Act itself does not apply to partnerships and sole traders, nor to many non-business entities. It is doubtful whether all the same accounting rules should apply to small local businesses as to large

---

22 Accounting Standards Board, *Statement of Principles for Financial Reporting*, 1999, p. 11.

multinational companies. Many people think the measurement principles should be the same even if smaller companies could be allowed to disclose less.

Some standards specifically exclude *smaller* entities, for example FRS 1 on Cash Flows, FRS 2 on Subsidiaries and SSAP 25's Net Asset disclosures. The Companies Act (Section 247) also makes this distinction where a company meets at least two of the following criteria:

	Small	*Medium*
Turnover (£ million)	< £5.6	< £22.8
Total assets (£ million)	< £2.8	< £11.4
Employees (number)	< 50	< 250

A 1994 working party[23] suggested exempting 'small' companies from all but five standards (SSAPs 4, 9, 13, 17 and 18) and UITF 7. That is, the working party thought it not worthwhile for small companies to follow *any* of the accounting standards issued since 1980. And Tweedie[24] has said: 'My own view is that we should not be in the business here [at the ASB] of setting standards for small companies.'

Entities applying the special FRS for Smaller Entities (FRSSE) are exempt from all other accounting standards, some of whose disclosure requirements it excludes. The latest FRSSE version comprises more than two hundred pages including nearly a hundred definitions.

---

23 CCAB Consultative Document, *Exemptions from Standards on Grounds of Size or Public Interest*, November 1994.

24 Derek Matthews and Jim Pirie, *The Auditors Talk: An Oral History of a Profession from the 1920's to the Present Day*, Garland Publishing, 2000, p. 387.

(ii) *Definitions* may partly overlap with scope: for example, SSAP 13 defines 'research' fairly narrowly. Some standards define key terms controversially: such as 'cash equivalents' in FRS 1, or 'extraordinary items' in FRS3, or 'residual value' in FRS 15, or 'current assets' in the Companies Act (Schedule 4, para. 77). For example, how the ASB's Statement of Principles defines 'asset' and 'liability' does not seem to fit goodwill and deferred tax respectively. This may be because the Statement of Principles is trying to define the 'matching' principle out of existence, which contradicts the traditional view[25] that 'the central purpose of accounting is to make possible the periodic matching of costs (efforts) and revenues (accomplishments)'.

(iii) *Presentation* rules cover the detailed *formats* for UK accounts (two basic formats to choose from for balance sheets, and four for profit and loss accounts). The 1981 Companies Act introduced these for the first time, as a result of the EEC's Fourth Directive, which itself stemmed from German accounting practice. Nobes[26] explains how 'under the National Socialists, the ascendant ideology of controlling the economy led naturally to the compulsory adoption of charts of accounts ...'

SSAP 5 on Value Added Tax (VAT) requires sales (turnover) to exclude VAT while amounts due from credit customers will normally include VAT. FRS 1 differs from IAS 7 in the specific format it requires for cash flow statements. FRS 3 requires a new

---

25 A. C. Littleton, *Structure of Accounting Theory*, AAA Monograph no. 5, Sarasota, FL, 1953.

26 C. W. Nobes, 'The Evolution of the Harmonising Provisions of the 1980 and 1981 Companies Acts', *Accounting and Business Research*, 53, winter 1983, p. 45.

statement of 'total recognised gains and losses' (known as STRGL), which FRED 22 suggests might in due course form part of a more comprehensive income statement.

Presentation may also cover *terminology*. British and US accounts contain very few identical terms. In the 'balance sheet' (statement of financial position) the terms 'cash' and 'current assets' are the same and not much else. The US layout may be horizontal rather than vertical. Even the date is not written in the same way: for instance, an English reader would normally interpret 9/11 as meaning the 9 November, not 11 September. In the 'profit and loss account' (income statement or operations statement or earnings statement) again many of the terms are different, from 'turnover' (sales revenue) to 'profit after tax' (net income). Despite all this, most people who understand British 'accounts' can also interpret US 'financial statements' without too much trouble.

(iv) *Disclosure* rules require companies to report certain matters in the accounts or in the notes or elsewhere in the annual report. These may stem from:

- the Companies Act: for example, turnover, purchases and disposals of fixed assets, details of tax expense, corresponding amounts for the previous year; or
- accounting standards: for example, deferred tax, pensions, cash flow statements; or
- the FSA's listing rules: for example, certain aspects of directors' pay.

Notes were not a legal requirement and were not a common

feature in accounts until the Companies Act 1948.[27] Since then UK practice has been to keep the main accounting statements relatively simple with much detail in the notes. And the extent of disclosure in the notes has increased greatly in recent years. Hobart Paper 128 noted that between 1973 and 1993 the number of pages of notes in three large companies' accounts virtually tripled: the General Electric Company (seven to twenty pages), Grand Metropolitan (six to twenty pages), and Imperial Chemical Industries (eight to 21 pages). Even more rapid expansion has occurred in the last ten years. As a result notes to the 2003 accounts of the following large companies comprised: GlaxoSmithKline 55 pages, Rio Tinto 44 pages, Unilever 47 pages. Outweighing all these is the annual report and accounts of HSBC Holdings plc, which totals 326 pages, including 107 pages of financial review and no fewer than 119 pages of notes.

Notes now often cover several pages each on topics such as: directors' pay, financial instruments, reconciliation to US accounting principles, retirement benefits, segment analysis. There must be an imminent danger here of over-kill. These super-abundant outpourings risk telling us more than we wish to know. Wilson et al., the authors of Ernst & Young's *UK GAAP*, say: 'The disclosure of directors' remuneration in the UK has become a bit of a nightmare. ... In some cases the sheer volume of information has become a barrier to effective communication.'[28] The same comments could well apply to financial instruments and retirement benefits too.

A bizarre US instance of a lengthy note comes to mind. Note 16

---

27 R. H. Parker, 'Harmonizing the notes in the UK and France', *European Accounting Review*, 5(2), 1996, p. 323.

28 Wilson et al., op. cit., p. 2,241 (sic).

to the 2001 Annual Report of Philip Morris (now Altria) covered *seven pages*. It related to the balance sheet item 'Contingencies', showing *no money amount* against that heading. This example reminds us that accounts, after all, are legal documents.

(v) *Measurement* is the final aspect covered by accounting standards (and, since 1981, to some extent by the Companies Act). Rules about the *basis of valuation*, for assets and liabilities or profit and loss, are often complex and may be controversial (see Chapter 6). Some of them can have a big effect on reported results: for example, goodwill and intangible assets (FRS 10); retirement benefits (FRS 17); deferred tax (FRS 19).

The Companies Act contains less on measurement than on disclosure but lays down rules about including only realised profits, valuing stocks at the lower of cost or net realisable value, and amortising goodwill. To some extent accounting standards conflict with each of these measurement rules in the Companies Act, all relating to the requirement for 'prudence' (see Appendix 3).

Another important aspect of measurement concerns the *unit of account*: for example, currency translation (SSAP 20); reflecting the effects of changing prices (IAS 15); and hyper-inflationary economies (IAS 29).

3 THE EMERGENCE OF INTERNATIONAL ACCOUNTING STANDARDS

International accounting has developed in the last thirty years to rival US accounting, where the FASB, backed by the SEC, sets standards serving the world's largest capital market. It is not yet clear whether there will be complete global convergence nor, if there is, whether it will be mainly on the basis of International Financial Reporting Standards (IFRS) or Generally Accepted Accounting Principles (US GAAP). The EU, which often seems to have an anti-American tendency in corporate matters, is requiring listed companies to apply IFRS from 2005.

Among important differences between relatively liberal IFRS and more authoritarian US GAAP have been:

- 'principles-based' standards versus very detailed regulations;
- 'true and fair' override versus strict compliance with US GAAP;
- general acceptance versus top-down imposition;
- alternative treatments allowed versus single treatment.

Accounting standards in the USA

American accounting derives from a similar legal background to British accounting. But US government agencies influence accounting standards, at least for listed companies, far more than in the UK. The Federal Trade Commission (FTC) was set up by the Clayton Antitrust Act of 1914, following the credit crisis of 1907, and the Securities and Exchange Commission emerged in 1934 as part of the US government's response to the Great Crash of 1929–32.

On each occasion the accounting profession had to deal with a government agency that had the formal power to take over its leading role. So in 1916 there was an agreement with the FTC on uniform accounting methods and in 1936 the American Institute of Certified Public Accountants set up a new Committee on Accounting Procedure (CAP), the first 'standard-setting' body, which aimed to narrow areas of difference in corporate reporting.

The CAP had about twenty part-time unpaid members, mostly in public practice. Its output, 51 advisory Accounting Research Bulletins (ARBs), listed practices that the SEC 'accepted' in filed accounts. In 1959 another AICPA committee, the Accounting Principles Board (APB), replaced it and published 31 Opinions. Its eighteen part-time unpaid members, now including some academics and business people, provided 'a change of name but little change of substance'.[1]

In the late 1960s a number of 'scandals' occurred which (as in the UK) led to new arrangements. The Financial Accounting Standards Board, with seven full-time paid members, succeeded the APB in 1973. In addition to extant ARBs and APB Opinions the FASB has issued over 140 Statements of Financial Accounting Standards, mostly very long and detailed. (US practice is to issue a new standard with a new number where the British amend

---

[1]	David Solomons, *Making Accounting Policy: The Quest for Credibility in Financial Reporting*, Oxford, 1986, p. 27.

an existing standard and retain the old number.) The two thick volumes of FASB standards and other pronouncements contain well over three thousand pages, together known as US GAAP. The FASB sets accounting standards in the USA, subject to 'veto-based delegation'[2] by the SEC; but the SEC enforces them. There is no doubt[3] which is the senior 'partner'.

There is some truth in the view that UK accounting standards (both SSAPs and FRSs) have tended to state broad principles and allow preparers to exercise a degree of judgement, while the FASB's US standards set out very detailed rigid prescriptions and permit few choices. Ultimately[4] this is a question of degree. But one common analogy used for US standards seems misguided: most 'cookbooks' allow plenty of room for flair and personal judgement. It is, however, possible to overstate the contrast: UK standards contain plenty of details too. Sir David Tweedie[5] has said that he would have preferred the ASB to limit itself to prin-ciples but that companies and auditing firms kept pressing to have the details spelt out. This may partly have been on account of potential litigation, which has been a much more serious threat in the USA, but some of this 'pressure' also stemmed from making UK standards *compulsory*.

Recently there has been another flurry of US 'scandals' (Enron, Worldcom, etc.) *despite* the existence of the SEC! Some of the trouble arose because companies and auditors did not always

2 Nahum A. Melumad and Toshiyuki Shibano, 'The SEC and the FASB: Regula-tion through Veto-Based Delegation', *Journal of Accounting Research*, 32(1), spring 1994, pp. 1–37.

3 See Paul B. W. Miller, *Accounting Horizons*, 16(3), September 2002, pp. 199–214.

4 Mark W. Nelson, *Accounting Horizons*, 17(1), March 2003, pp. 91–2.

5 Sir David Tweedie, in Mumford and Peasnell, op. cit., p. xxiv.

follow US GAAP, but sometimes they did obey standards, which were faulty. In consequence the 2002 Sarbanes-Oxley Act was rushed through in an attempt to 'tighten up requirements' further in several areas. As so often when regulation falls short of what it promises, the 'solution' is to reinforce failure by more of the same.

In the USA 'presenting fairly' requires absolute compliance with US GAAP even if it might lead to a misleading view. There is no provision in law or in practice for any equivalent of the UK's true and fair 'override'. The SEC has recently announced[6] a move from a 'rules-based' approach towards one that is more 'principles-based' (Sarbanes-Oxley required the SEC to study whether this was feasible). Such a change would involve serious technical problems[7] and seems unlikely to happen. A culture of issuing orders[8] is hard to change.

These recent US scandals have been a huge embarrassment to the SEC and the FASB. Just when there is pressure for worldwide convergence the US 'investor protection' rules have evidently not worked as advertised. So the previous American argument, that everyone else should converge with the supposedly 'high-quality' US system, now looks much less credible. How fortunate that we did not all 'harmonise' a few years ago on the basis of the US standards, as no doubt some 'experts' would have wished. What a good thing that competition between rival standards still allows at least some choice between different approaches. But European

---

6   *Financial Times*, 26/27 July 2003.

7   See Maines et al., 'Evaluating Concepts-based vs Rules-based Approaches to Standard Setting', *Accounting Horizons*, 17(1), March 2003, pp. 73–89.

8   See Katherine Schipper, 'Principle-based Accounting Standards', *Accounting Horizons*, 17(1), March 2003, pp. 61–72.

(or British) *schadenfreude* would be inappropriate. With respect to accounting regulation *all* countries have plenty of room for improvement.

The European Union

British company law goes back more than 150 years, and the Americans have had accounting standards for seventy years. In contrast the Fourth and Seventh Company Law Directives (the main ones affecting accounts) have been in place in most EU countries for fewer than twenty years. Before that European governments had often dictated accounting rules to meet fiscal or planning objectives.

The Fourth Directive in 1974 adopted the British aim for 'a true and fair view' as an overriding requirement for company accounts in all member states. (The original expert group had been asked[9] to report on the harmonisation of accounts for *listed* companies only.) This was a great compliment to the high quality of British accounting, which at that time had evolved with hardly any influence from 'accounting standards' as such.

But 'it is impossible to translate the words true and fair literally into any other Community language ...'[10] Indeed, EU member states other than Ireland and the UK even use somewhat different words. They seem to fall into three groups – German, Scandinavian, and southern Europe and Benelux:

---

9   Peter Walton, 'The true and fair view and the drafting of the Fourth Directive', *European Accounting Review*, 6(4), 1997, p. 722.

10   Karel van Hulle, 'The true and fair view override in the European Accounting Directives', *European Accounting Review*, 6(4), 1997, p. 716.

- Austria and Germany: translated as 'a picture in accordance with the facts';
- Denmark, Finland and Sweden: translated as 'a right-looking picture';
- Benelux, France, Greece, Italy, Portugal and Spain: translated as 'a faithful picture'.

'There is no European consensus on what a "true and fair view" means or implies.'[11] For instance, while International Accounting Standards (IAS) allowed the Last In First Out (LIFO) method of valuing stock it is very rare in the UK. Even though the overriding concept of 'a true and fair view' legally applies throughout the European Union not all countries interpret it in the same way. The seemingly identical requirement may mislead readers to expect accounts in different EU countries to be more alike than they really are.

Flower and Ebbers say: '[I]n financial reporting, the differences within the EU are greater than the differences between certain EU states and the rest of the world ... Britain is closer to the USA than it is to France, and Germany is closer to Japan than it is to the Netherlands.'[12] A useful distinction[13] may be between 'common law' countries (Britain and its former colonies) and 'code-law' countries (such as France, Germany and Japan), as a proxy for the extent of market versus political influence on financial reporting.

Even within single nation-states there can be variations. The

---

11 David Alexander and Simon Archer, *The European Accounting Guide*, Academic Press, London, 1992, p. 20.

12 John Flower with Gabi Ebbers, *Global Financial Reporting*, Palgrave, 2002, p. 211.

13 Ray Ball, S. P. Kothari and Ashok Robin, 'The effect of international institutional factors on properties of accounting earnings', *Journal of Accounting and Economics*, 29, 2000, pp. 1–51.

union between England and Scotland occurred in 1707, nearly three hundred years ago, yet their legal systems still differ. A more up-to-date example would be 'one country, two systems', the fifty-year undertaking by China in 1997 with respect to Hong Kong. In continental Europe too there are important business and other differences between West and East Germany and between the north and south of Italy.

Between them the US and UK stock markets represent more than 60 per cent of the total market capitalisation of all listed equity shares worldwide.[14] Capital market pressures have strongly influenced accounts in both countries and institutional investors are very important, though single pension funds hardly ever own a large percentage of any one company's shares. In much of continental Europe, however, few pensions are funded. Family-owned companies and inter-corporate ownership of equity shares are widespread while publicly quoted and traded companies are much less common. Concentrated voting power may serve the interests of committed long-term investors[15] but controlling owners may also have access to private sources of information. Hence in Europe there may have been less pressure to improve the quality of published financial statements.

The European Union's company law directives were intended mainly to protect current members (shareholders) and third parties such as creditors. According to Van Hulle (1989): '[Poten-

---

14 *Financial Times*, 2 February 2004. As at 31 December 2003, Wall Street represented 52 per cent and London 10 per cent. The other main components were: ex-British colonies (other than the USA) 7 per cent; the twelve eurozone countries 14 per cent; Japan 9 per cent; Switzerland 3 per cent; rest of the world 5 per cent.

15 See the introductory chapter by M. Becht and C. Mayer in Fabrizio Barca and Marco Becht (eds), *The Control of Corporate Europe*, Oxford University Press, 2001.

tial] investor protection is not the primary objective ... In this respect, the approach that the [EU] follows must be distinguished from the capital market approach which is the basis for accounting standard setting in other parts of the world.'[16] Similarly: 'The object of group accounts is not, primarily, to inform the proprietors, the shareholders or the financial markets or enable them to take buy or sell decisions ...'[17]

For some years an important question has been whether the EU should attempt to develop its own accounting standards. But there was little support for this and instead the EU has decided that from 2005 listed companies in all member states must adopt International Accounting Standards. Hence Van Hulle recently said: '[this] implies a change in mentality for many EU countries. Financial reporting will have to move away from conservative tax-oriented reporting to a system whereby the needs of investors (and other stakeholders) are the primary focus'.[18]

So-called conservative accounting can have surprising results. For example, in 1993 Daimler-Benz for the first time restated its accounts, prepared under German accounting principles, in line with US GAAP. The result was to *reduce* reported profit, although many observers had expected German accounting principles to be 'more conservative' than US ones. But 1993 had been a 'bad' year, which Daimler-Benz improved for accounting purposes by drawing on secret reserves set aside in earlier years.

---

16 Karel van Hulle, 'The EC experience of harmonization', *Accountancy*, 10, October 1989.

17 Professor Wymeersch, 1980, quoted (and translated) by Tom Watts, 'British Accounting Standards and the EEC', in Bryan Carsberg and Susan Dev (eds), *External Financial Reporting*, Prentice-Hall for the London School of Economics and Political Science, 1984, p. 144.

18 Karel van Hulle, Introduction to Wilson et al., op. cit.

In some areas EU accounting requirements may be more stringent than IAS: for example, the Fourth Directive requires specific formats for balance sheets and income statements. Thus merely 'complying' with IAS will not always suffice for companies in EU member states, which must also obey the law. After expansion the EU will become a more heterogeneous collective with about half of its 25 member states having much smaller economies and financial markets (the ten countries joining in 2004 have a combined gross domestic product only about one quarter of that of the UK alone).

A private sector grouping called the European Financial Reporting Advisory Group (EFRAG) will help the EU's Accounting Regulatory Committee (ARC) to decide whether or not to endorse future International Financial Reporting Standards (IFRS). Such endorsement, which is intended to provide political backing for international accounting standards, is by no means certain. One could indeed argue that the EU itself lacks democratic legitimacy. And until the Court of Auditors feels able to approve the European Commission's own accounts, which it has now declined to do for nine years running, the EU probably lacks some moral authority in accounting too.

The International Accounting Standards Board

The International Accounting Standards Committee was started in 1973 with accounting bodies from nine countries. From 1983 the IASC's members included all the professional bodies that were members of the International Federation of Accountants (IFAC). By 2001 there were 153 members from 112 countries. There was then a major structural change leading to the new International Accounting Standards Board (IASB).

British accountants have always been prominent in the IASC. Sir Henry Benson (of Cooper Brothers) was the key founder in 1973; its headquarters are in London; and the three most recent leaders have been British: David Cairns, Sir Bryan Carsberg and Sir David Tweedie. Apart from a permanent secretary-general, other staff members were seconded on short-term assignments from various audit firms and other bodies.

In 1980 Nobes[19] produced a well-known scheme of different countries' accounting practices which by now is somewhat out of date. His main distinction was between 'bottom-up', commercial, judgemental systems (US, UK, ex-British colonies and the Netherlands) and 'top-down', government, statutory systems (France, Spain, Germany and Japan).

Although the IASC 'originally hoped for mandatory status'[20] it has no means of enforcing its standards (listed in Appendix 2). Until fairly recently most of the IASC's standards tended to follow either UK or US standards, often allowing more than one method of accounting. The IASC influenced many countries in eastern Europe. And many developing countries adopted IAS more or less wholesale, subject possibly to certain local adjustments.

In 1993 the IASC revised ten standards with a substantial reduction of options. The labels 'benchmark' and 'allowed alternative', where they remain, are of equal status: they imply no preference for 'benchmark' treatments. Instead of endorsing all these revised standards, as had been hoped, the International Organisation of Securities Commissions (IOSCO) (formed in 1986) asked for further changes to two of them and for new standards in other

---

19 Christopher W. Nobes, 'A judgmental international classification of financial reporting practices', *Journal of Business Finance and Accounting*, spring 1983.
20 Christopher W. Nobes, *British Accounting Review*, 22(1), March 1990, p. 42.

areas. The IASC continues to tolerate alternatives in several areas, its view being that there can be *more than one* acceptable accounting treatment. The new IASB regime may not share this view, which the SEC opposes.

A 1995 survey[21] showed how different countries handled various accounting topics and which countries followed and which diverged from IAS. Australia seemed closest to the IASC line, followed in order by Spain, Canada, Sweden, the United States, the Netherlands, the United Kingdom, Switzerland, Japan, Germany and Italy. But many countries (including the UK) have changed their accounting practices considerably in the past decade or so.

In 1995 the IASC and IOSCO embarked on another project aiming at getting IASC to upgrade many of its standards (some did not need it). The idea was again for IOSCO to endorse IAS for cross-border capital-raising and listing purposes in all global markets. The IASC completed its work in December 1998, and in May 2000 IOSCO announced the result of its review of the thirty 'core' standards. Instead of endorsing the package, however, IOSCO set out other ways to permit the use of IAS, either reconciling to some different accounting treatment or by supplemental disclosures.

The IASC has enjoyed two advantages over UK and US standard-setters, which it may be about to lose: it may be worth noting that some people would regard these 'advantages' as drawbacks. Its accounting standards were *voluntary*, in that the IASC itself could not enforce them: hence they genuinely depended on *general acceptance*. And in several areas they currently allow *more than one* accounting treatment (as does the ASB in a few areas).

---

21   Price Waterhouse, *Survey of International Accounting Practices*, 1995.

This relatively liberal attitude towards standards contrasts with the more authoritarian US approach which the new IASB seems in some danger of following.

As from April 2001 the IASB replaced the IASC and will call its future standards IFRS rather than IAS. It will have some fifteen full-time professional staff, compared with the SEC's much larger total staff. Of the board's fourteen initial members:

- twelve are full-time;
- five had been full-time standard-setters, four executives in multinational companies, three partners in audit firms, and two academics;
- ten are from 'Anglo-Saxon' countries, five from European countries (including two UK);
- only two could be described[22] mainly as 'users' of accounts (even though the IASC's constitution calls for at least three).

A key feature of the new arrangements is that IFRSs will require the backing of no more than eight out of the fourteen members, a bare majority. This allows for a much larger element of 'disagreement' than most standard-setters. And on paper it seems possible for the ten 'Anglo-Saxon' members to vote through a standard with which the French, German, Swiss and Japanese members all disagree. (Of course, the mix of members' nationalities may vary over time.) Putting it bluntly, at least in theory, in the future the IFRS may not enjoy 'general acceptance' even within the IASB itself.

---

22   According to Flower and Ebbers, op. cit., p. 258.

International harmonisation

Depending on how it is presented, the process of harmonisation can be taken to mean different things: 'I harmonise, you standardise, he imposes rules'.

- I try to allow readers to compare the accounts of different companies;
- you discourage alternative ways of accounting for similar transactions;
- he forces many different kinds of business into a single accounting straitjacket.

These are three different ways of viewing the process of harmonisation, which resonate in different ways.

The verb 'to harmonise' means: 'to add notes to a melody to produce harmony'. But another definition may be more apt: 'to bring into harmony' (meaning agreement). It seems there is more than one meaning of 'harmonisation'. Could there also be more than one 'true and fair view' of a company's financial position and performance? If so, perhaps caution is needed in trying to 'harmonise' the accounting requirements of different companies of different sizes in different industries in different countries at different stages of development.

People sometimes suggest that if all companies were to produce accounts in accordance with a single set of accounting standards that would reduce their cost of capital. If this were true there would be an incentive for companies to fall into line of their own accord with *no need for compulsion*. But the evidence[23] does

---

23 *Improving business reporting – a customer focus: meeting the information needs of investors and creditors*, 'Comprehensive report of the (Jenkins) Special Committee on Financial reporting', AICPA, 1993.

not 'present an empirical case that informative disclosure lowers the cost of capital'.

Botosan[24] examined 122 US machinery firms, distinguishing 62 smaller firms, which nine or fewer analysts followed, from sixty larger firms with ten or more analysts. She compiled a 'disclosure score' from the contents of each annual report and concluded there was *no evidence* of any link between disclosure level and the cost of equity capital for firms with a high analyst following. Since this is the type of firm that international accounting harmonisation is most likely to affect, her work appears to provide *zero support* for it. More recent research by the same author on a much larger scale[25] found that 'greater total disclosure is not associated with a lower cost of equity capital'.

In the last few decades multinational companies and large worldwide accounting firms have been moving towards some gradual convergence in accounting practices around the world. Even in the absence of focused coercive efforts in this direction from leading standard-setters, one might expect a tendency for such a natural spontaneous process of voluntary evolution to continue.

Readers of the accounts of multinational companies may have to cope with different currencies, different legal systems and different industries – as well as, of course, different languages (unless the IASB is proposing that all accounts be produced in Esperanto). So it is not obvious why people claim it is so important

---

24   Christine Botosan, 'The Disclosure Level and the Cost of Equity Capital', *Accounting Review*, July 1997.
25   Christine A. Botosan and Marlene A. Plumlee, 'A Re-examination of Disclosure Level and the Expected Cost of Equity Capital', *Journal of Accounting Research*, 40(1), March 2002, pp. 21–40.

to 'harmonise' international accounting practices (or 'standardise' them: in practice the two words seem to mean much the same). As Warren Buffet says: 'The business world is simply too complex for a single set of rules to effectively describe economic reality for all enterprises ...'[26] In a troublesome set of accounts, moreover, drafting the narrative can sometimes be as difficult as computing the figures,[27] which has obvious implications when translating foreign accounts.

Not only may effective harmonisation be difficult but there is a question of whether it is even desirable. Once one gets away from the flawed notion that annual accounts are regular prospectuses the benefits seem less enticing. 'It is difficult to reconcile harmonisation with too much individual freedom.'[28]

There is a big difference between the spontaneous emergence of 'general acceptance' of certain rules in a number of areas and a deliberate attempt to establish what, in effect, would be a global monopoly. Thus failure to achieve international agreement on a single set of standards would by no means be a disaster. It would simply mean competition between standards, which is perfectly healthy. Indeed, Solomons noted: 'The arguments for harmonisation across countries are much the same as the arguments for having accounting standards within a single country.'[29] We now turn to this issue.

---

26 Lawrence A. Cunningham, *The Essays of Warren Buffet: Lessons for Investors and Managers*, John Wiley, 2002, p. 223.

27 A. M. C. Morison, 'The Role of the Reporting Accountant Today', in Baxter and Davidson (eds), *Studies in Accounting Theory*, Sweet & Maxwell, London, 3rd edition, 1977, p. 272.

28 Karel van Hulle and K. U. Leuven, *European Accounting Review*, 2(1), May 1993, p. 101.

29 Solomons, *Making Accounting Policy*, op. cit., p. 62.

4 ARGUMENTS FOR ACCOUNTING STANDARDS

Both Solomons[1] and the Dearing Committee[2] acknowledged that not everyone favours accounting standards, but it is not always easy to find clear statements of the arguments for and against. This chapter discusses six arguments *for* accounting standards and Chapter 5 discusses four arguments *against*.

Six arguments for accounting standards are:

- dishonesty of preparers of accounts;
- lack of independence of auditors;
- possible damage to investors;
- complexity of accounting decisions;
- uniform words and layout;
- helping users to compare the accounts of different companies.

Dishonesty of preparers of accounts

Agents providing an account of their stewardship may well prefer to present a rosy picture rather than a gloomy one. There may therefore be a conflict of interest between preparers and users of accounts. Hence 'the major thrust of accounting standards is to

---

1   Solomons, 'The Political Implications', op. cit.
2   Dearing, op. cit., p.7.

reduce the freedom of preparers in order to satisfy some of the demands of the users.'[3]

The Dearing Committee[4] mentioned two specific sources of pressures which 'must tend in some cases' to influence the judgement of preparers of accounts: 'the concern to maintain or enhance a listed company's share price to safeguard against or to launch takeovers; and the trend towards rewarding managements through profit-sharing and share-option schemes'.

In effect the suggestion is that some preparers of accounts may be less than honest. This may mean reluctance to make full disclosure, not necessarily willingness to make false disclosure. Hence agency theory[5] proposes regular audits by independent accountants as a way to monitor agents' actions in the interests both of managers and of shareholders. It pays insiders to provide assurance to outsiders. Audits will not detect every fraud, but nor will regulation prevent all wrongdoing.

Companies (other than certain small ones) have to publish regular audited reports and many equity investors continue to own shares for long periods. So in the long run honesty may be the best policy. Even if dishonesty might seem to 'pay' in an ephemeral relationship where you are never going to meet someone again, it could be clearly unwise if one expects a more permanent involvement.[6] This may partly explain the difference in regulatory atti-

---

3   J. A. Burggraaff, 'The political dimensions of accounting standards setting in Europe', in M. Bromwich and A. Hopwood (eds), *Accounting Standard Setting: An International Perspective*, Pitman, 1983, p. 4.

4   Dearing, op. cit., p. 11.

5   Michael C. Jensen and William H. Meckling, 'Theory of the firm: managerial behaviour, agency costs and ownership structure', *Journal of Financial Economics*, 3, 1976.

6   See Robert Axelrod, *The Evolution of Cooperation*, Basic Books, New York, 1984.

tudes between London and New York. At one time everyone knew almost everyone else (and their families) in the City of London, hence the stock exchange could flourish with the motto 'My word is my bond'. The long-term social penalty for cheating could be devastating. Not so in New York, which was a much less settled society.

There can be stock-market-related pressure on managers of listed companies to meet an external target for short-term reported earnings. But there may be a danger of crossing the fuzzy line between quasi-legitimate income-smoothing and deception. A recent report[7] that far more companies beat quarterly earnings estimates by a penny than miss them by a penny suggests an element of manipulation. The best solution, if it were possible, would be to remove the pressure on managers to commit to specific short-term earnings targets. No business can honestly be expected to predict its annual profit or loss to within a tiny margin of error, still less its quarterly earnings. Perhaps stock exchanges or professional accountancy bodies should discourage such dangerous and potentially distorting estimates.

Recent accounting standards have injected a further huge dose of volatility into profits that were already unpredictable. By chance they may thus have diminished the unhealthy pressures on management to pretend to predict the uncertain future and then (perhaps) be tempted to fake the results. A similar problem bedevils top management remuneration. In this case it is the short-term aspect which causes much of the trouble. If senior managers are meant to be setting strategy for years ahead it makes little sense

---

7   *Financial Times*, 27 February 2004. See also Richard Zeckhauser, François Degeorge and Javendu Patel, 'Earnings Management to Exceed Thresholds', *Journal of Business*, Jan. 1999, Vol. 72, issue 1, pp. 1–33.

to base a large part of their pay on fallible short-term measures of company performance.

Evidence to the Cohen Committee[8] suggested: '… there are in the City three classes – … the perfectly honest people, the entirely dishonest people, and an intermediate class who are prepared to be dishonest and shady if it is not too difficult or dangerous … these latter form a very large proportion of wrongdoers, and … legislation [providing for more complete disclosure] would be very effective in deterring them'.

Disclosure requirements are one thing but *measurement* standards that require or rule out certain accounting treatments are quite another. They can reduce the range of choice about how to provide 'a true and fair view'. Forbidding company directors to use their own judgement may indeed reduce the 'pressure' on them, but that is not to say it will result in accounts of higher quality.

Lack of independence of auditors

Dearing said: 'it would be idealistic to assume that all auditors at all times are unmindful of the risk of losing business'. This implies that some auditors too are dishonest or at best pusillanimous. But in an oral history[9] of the UK auditing profession it was striking how many of the 68 accountants interviewed played down this point. In practice, they said, the risk of losing an audit carried hardly any weight, at least in those days. Even today a large auditing firm might well not care about losing specific clients. But an individual partner in charge of a particular audit

---

8   D. M. Emanuel and I. C. Stewart (eds), *Essays in Honour of Trevor R. Johnston*, University of Auckland, 1981, p. 28.

9   Matthews and Pirie, op. cit.

might be much more sensitive about the prospect of losing one of 'his' or 'her' clients.

The existence of accounting standards may lessen two different kinds of pressures on auditors: client companies threatening to shop around for more congenial audit opinions and possible lawsuits for negligence. It makes sense to talk of 'client companies' even though some purists argue that the client is not a company's management but its shareholders.

Reducing the scope for judgement can reduce the risk in auditing. Fear of litigation may partly explain why auditing firms press for ever more detail in accounting standards. Auditors might have a sound defence against a lawsuit for negligence if they could show that a company's accounts have complied precisely with detailed rules. Otherwise it might be harder to convince a court that an auditing firm's judgement was not negligent. The more general the rules the more room for doubt.

According to Fama: 'Like the outside directors, the outside auditors are policed by the market for their services which prices them in large part on the basis of how well they resist perverting the interests of one set of factors (e.g. security holders) to the benefit of other factors (e.g. management). Like the professional outside director, the welfare of the outside auditor depends largely on "reputation".'[10] Indeed, Hayek says more broadly that 'competition is in large measure competition for reputation'.[11]

If audit firms merely tick boxes to record compliance with standard rules they cannot easily distinguish themselves by the

---

10   Eugene Fama, 'Agency Problems and the Theory of the Firm', *Journal of Political Economy*, 88(2), 1980.

11   F. A. Hayek, 'The Meaning of Competition', in *Individualism and Economic Order*, Routledge & Kegan Paul, London, 1949, p. 97.

quality of their judgement, in which case perhaps a reputation for *competence* hardly matters. But the awful example of what happened to Arthur Andersen underlines what can happen if an auditing firm's *independence* comes into question. Other leading firms, though, have also been found guilty of serious lapses in the recent past and have had to pay substantial sums by way of damages to litigants. It is not clear whether this has much damaged *their* names (a recent study[12] suggested not). Perhaps all accounting firms are now tarred with the same brush.

It is unlikely to be in a *company*'s long-run interests to deceive its own members, though directors might take a shorter-term view. Setting up audit committees comprising only non-executive directors tries to guard against this. Nor probably would *auditors* gain in the long run if they abetted any such attempt. This does not guarantee the complete absence of short-term deception in accounts, but it is doubtful whether any other approach could do so either.

Possible damage to investors

Solomons stresses potential damage to investors:

> Managers may have more to gain by withholding information than from disclosing it. We cannot depend on the market to discipline promptly companies that are free to choose what and how to report to investors. Even if good accounting can be relied on to drive out bad in the long run, investors may suffer too much damage in the short run to permit freedom from regulation.[13]

---

12 Clive S. Lennox, 'Audit Quality and Auditor Size', *Journal of Business Finance and Accounting*, Sept./Oct. 1999, pp. 779–805.

13 Solomons, 'The Political Implications', op. cit., p. 107 (adapted).

This suggests that standards should require (or at least encourage) both minimum levels of disclosure and specific methods of measurement. But is there much evidence of any 'damage' due to absence of regulation? And by 'investors' do we mean *existing* shareholders in companies (which is what British company law has in mind) or also *potential* investors (which US regulators have always aimed at)? There is also the question of whether we are mainly concerned with long-term investors or with short-term speculators. It is not clear why we should seek to provide special protection for the latter; nor is it evident that accounting standards will provide much help to the former.

Certainly there were some accounting frauds in the old days, just as there are now. The SEC was set up in 1934 as a response to the Great Crash of 1929. It has been claimed[14] that in the pre-SEC period vast amounts of money were lost: '… misuse of insider information, and other types of manipulation and fraud, which frequently relied on the deliberate use of manipulation and the absence of full disclosure, were widespread in the pre-SEC period … and seem less prevalent today'. Yet though some *prospectuses* may certainly have been misleading, Benston says[15] there was little evidence of investor losses due to poor or misleading company *accounts*.

Between 1945 and 1969 the ICAEW issued Recommendations to its members, while the Scottish Institute preferred not to. But no one suggests that Scottish company accounts were therefore of

---

14   Marshall E. Blume and Irwin Friend, *The Changing Role of the Individual Investor*, John Wiley & Sons, 1978, p. 203 (quoted in Alex Berenson, *The Number*, Simon & Schuster, 2003, p. 138).

15   George J. Benston, *Corporate financial disclosure in the UK and the USA*, Saxon House, Farnborough, Hants., 1976, p. 19.

lower quality than English ones. So is there any reason to suppose that the absence of accounting standards after 1970 would have damaged UK investors?

Asymmetric information, which company directors may possess but shareholders may not, will always be a potential problem. But apart from requiring regular publication there is another way to get stock markets to reflect any relevant news that company managers possess. That is to permit 'insider trading' by managers in their own companies' shares, which could make stock market prices better guides to value for the investing public. Hence it is not obvious why stopping insider trading, if it were possible, would increase 'confidence' in markets.

It has been suggested[16] that without full disclosure by legal compulsion the check on how well companies use retained profits is likely to be too weak. But why should this be the law's concern? Another, better way to control the use of profits might be to let *shareholders* vote to *increase* dividends above what company directors recommend. Such action by the owners would then reduce retained profits.

Modern portfolio theory says that by holding a number of different shares investors can diversify away much of any company's unique risk. In other words, putting all your eggs in one basket (even if you keep a sharp eye on the basket) is unnecessarily risky. The same argument might apply to having only a single global setter of accounting standards!

So while accounts might help assess a particular company's total risk, pretending to analyse the backward-looking accounts of specific companies in detail plays hardly any part in the process of

16   Rose, op. cit., p. 16.

building a suitable equity portfolio. There is little reason to think that 'fundamental analysis' is useful for forward-looking investment decisions either for existing or for potential shareholders. Nor are accounts by any means the only source of information for shareholders or stock markets: indeed, accounts are usually neither the most important nor the most up-to-date source.

Complexity of accounting decisions

Another suggested reason for accounting standards is the complexity of the decisions facing preparers and auditors of accounts. But if some preparers of accounts or some auditors need help, voluntary guidelines could provide it, which is what Dearing actually suggested. There is no need to *tell* them what to do. Indeed, the preparation of such guidelines could be regarded as a fundamental aspect of a professional body's work.

It may be useful for accounting bodies to advise their members on technical aspects of preparing accounts. Their members can then choose whether to agree with the 'advice' or not. Relying on authority to compel truth can be dangerous, as the examples of Nazi mathematics[17] and Soviet biology[18] from the last century remind us. The same is true of accounting. As Morison said: 'Differing opinions reflect difficult problems, which do not cease to be difficult just because one party to the debate has been outlawed.'[19]

In some respects standard-setters themselves may have made accounting measurement more complex: for example, FRS 17 on

---

17   Karl Dietrich Bracher, *The German Dictatorship*, Penguin, 1973, p. 335.

18   Carl J. Friedrich and Zbigniew Brzezinski, *Totalitarian Dictatorship and Autocracy*, Praeger, 1966, p. 150.

19   A. M. C. Morison, in Baxter and Davidson, op. cit., p. 279.

Retirement Benefits, IAS 39 on Measurement of Financial Instruments, or SFAS 109 on Tax. And the ASB discussion paper on goodwill proposed a valuation method called 'Capitalisation and Annual Review' which contained an extremely complex fifteen-page appendix. But standard-setters would probably argue both that their standards reflect the complexity of the real world and that they are responding to pressures from auditors.

The ASB sometimes complicates presentation too, as in FRS 1 on Cash Flow Statements or FRS 3's hard-to-follow profit-and-loss account layout, though again standard-setters would argue that these layouts attempt to cope with complex realities. The same standard's Statement of Total Recognised Gains and Losses more or less duplicates the details of changes in reserves which the Companies Act already requires. The danger is that if the ASB were to incorporate the STRGL into a single overall 'income statement', companies could be reporting unrealised gains as profits. The Companies Act has good reasons for expressly forbidding this, and unrealised profits would also form a poor basis on which to establish tax assessments (another of the purposes of company accounts).

Accounting can be difficult both because of its technical character, which combines economic and legal concepts, and because of the intricate nature of modern business. Yet mandatory accounting standards limit the freedom of company directors and auditors to exercise discretion. The more complex the task, the stronger the need for independent judgement and the weaker the case for top-down regulation.

Uniform words and layout

It is claimed: 'Uniformity, both of words and layout, can help reduce the "semantic noise" which obstructs the clarity of the message.'[20] But this seems rather a minor point: most British readers can follow American balance sheets even though the format is different and almost the only common terms are 'current assets' and 'cash'. It is somewhat ironic that the EU should feel it necessary to dictate which English words to use in UK company accounts. After all, companies in other member states are using Danish, Dutch, Finnish, French, German, Greek, Italian, Portuguese, Spanish and Swedish – with Czech, Estonian, Hungarian, Latvian, Lithuanian, Maltese, Polish, Slovak and Slovene now as well.

There is little need for standards to *impose* uniform words and layout. Where this makes sense it tends to happen anyway without any need for compulsion. For example, 'prospectuses in the UK [fell] (voluntarily) into a reasonably uniform format because users liked it that way'.[21] And does it really matter if such convergence falls short of complete uniformity?

Any official system of language is likely to freeze practice and can be positively harmful. Most English people know two examples, one sinister and the other laughable. In Orwell's *Nineteen Eighty-four* 'Newspeak' tried to stamp out freedom and restrict thought, while the Académie Française attempts vainly to 'purify' French. (Rather than '*le PE ratio*' a Ministerial Commission of Economic and Financial Terminology[22] apparently prefers '*le coefficient de*

20 Peter Bird, as quoted by Solomons, 'The Political Implications', op. cit., p. 108.
21 Tom Watts, in Carsberg and Dev, op. cit., p. 140.
22 R. H. Parker, 'European languages of account', *European Accounting Review*, 10(1), 2001, p. 144.

capitalisation des résultats', and in place of '*cash flow*' the bureau-crats decree '*marge brute d'autofinancement*'.)

The Fourth Directive replaced 'current liabilities' as a stand-alone item with 'creditors: amounts falling due within one year'. Was there any reason to think people failed to understand such a well-known term before it was outlawed? Presumably not, for the line after 'net current assets' now reads: 'total assets less current liabili-ties'. So the term 'current liabilities' lives on, just as well understood as before – or perhaps less well understood for the casual reader given that the terminology is now *required* to be inconsistent.

For another example, stemming from the Seventh Directive, the 1989 Companies Act, in amending the 1985 Act, states: 'For "related companies", wherever occurring in any other context [than "shares in related companies"], substitute "undertakings in which the company has a participating interest".' Do we really need this kind of edict? Here the change requires nine words in place of two, twenty syllables instead of six. The required expres-sion seems much clumsier than the one it replaces. So why *compel* everyone to make the change?

Another important question arises: how do we expect gradual improvements over time to occur? We can hardly assume that we have now reached perfection. But even if we had, future conditions will be different. Both the Fourth and the Seventh Directives are now somewhat out of date. But it would probably take many years for the EU to issue new instructions and much longer still for every member state to amend its company law: Italy was eleven years late in implementing the Fourth Directive. Natural changes in language can occur much more quickly than that and with much less fuss. To use a notorious British accounting term, language evolves *flexibly*.

Even young children understand the rules of grammar without being able to express them clearly in words. We know more than we can say. Yet no single person or committee decided on the rules and imposed them (even in France!). Nor does anyone have to get 'permission' to *change* language. It happens spontaneously. Why not let accounting, the 'language of business', evolve similarly?

Helping users to compare the accounts of different companies

There is a view that the public expects companies' accounts to be accurate and comparable with each other. 'How do you explain to an intelligent public that two companies in the same industry can follow different accounting principles and both get a true and fair audit report?'[23] Solomons says: 'The value of the information which each company provides to its shareholders is much enhanced if it is easy to compare with other companies' accounts. So regulation is needed to secure what everyone wants.'[24]

According to Sprouse: 'The quest for comparability is a large part of what standard setting is about.'[25] Indeed, Zeff[26] says the SEC has always seen the freedom to use alternative accounting practices as incompatible with comparability among corporations' financial statements.

According to a US standard-setter:

---

23 Michael Lafferty, 'Why It Is Time for Another Leap Forward', *Accountancy*, January 1979.

24 Solomons, 'The Political Implications', op. cit., p. 107 (adapted). See also Schipper, op. cit., p. 62.

25 Robert Sprouse, quoted in Bromwich, op. cit., p. 301.

26 Stephen A. Zeff, *Accounting Horizons*, March 1995, pp. 52–70.

> The difficulty in making financial comparisons between enterprises because of the use of different accounting methods has been accepted for many years as the principal reason for the development of accounting standards. Indeed, the only other possible reason for wanting accounting standards would be a belief that there was one right method among the available alternatives, and few people, if any, hold such a belief.[27]

In the absence of accounting standards similar companies might choose to adopt different accounting treatments. So it is tempting for regulators to want to forbid differences that might otherwise emerge and persist. But although standard-setters may have tried to narrow the differences between different companies' accounts, genuine comparability between them may be hard to achieve. Standards sometimes recognise this, for example in allowing companies to use their own regional definitions for segment-reporting purposes.

Some people demand uniformity and rigid rules: '… so that security analysts and others can look at the numbers and delude themselves into thinking that they are comparing the operating results and performances of unrelated and wholly different companies. [But] such comparisons are just not feasible'.[28]

Those who do not regard valuation as one of the main purposes of accounts may not much care about comparing different companies' accounts. Indeed, users seem to value information that is consistent over time more highly.[29] Certainly, comparing results

---

27 Cheri L. Reither, 'How the FASB Approaches a Standard-setting Issue', *Accounting Horizons*, 11(4), December 1997, p. 94.

28 Hornstobel, op. cit., p. 79.

29 (Jenkins) Special Committee, op. cit.

over time within one enterprise is much easier. More than forty years ago I examined[30] the accounts of the five main American cigarette companies over the period 1951–62. But comparing the financial results of the different companies directly was rarely possible even though they made almost identical products. Many of the reasons still exist today.

Even without anybody imposing or suggesting accounting standards, a number of accounting conventions might emerge which almost everyone would accept. That is how the famous convention of prudence evolved. Hence accounting standards may neither be necessary to achieve a good deal of similarity in accounting nor sufficient to prevent quite a lot of difference.

---

30   D. R. Myddelton, *The Comparability of Published Financial Statements*, unpublished research report, Harvard Business School, 1963.

5 ARGUMENTS AGAINST ACCOUNTING STANDARDS

The four arguments in this chapter against accounting standards deal with:

- stifling or forbidding independent judgement by accountants;
- reducing competition in ideas and stopping or distorting evolution and experiment;
- legitimising bad accounting (and sometimes forbidding good accounting);
- misleading the public by unduly raising expectations.

All these imply long-term consequences, which may not always be the immediate concern of standard-setters, politicians or the public.

Stifling independent judgement

If you have to do what you're told, why bother to think for yourself? Stalin is supposed to have been asked once whether he preferred people to do what he wanted because they were afraid of him or because they really agreed with his views. He replied that he preferred people who obeyed him out of fear since those who agreed with him might change their minds!

Baxter long ago pointed out how the existence of standards can impose heavy pressures on an auditor:

Suppose that the medical profession's first dislike
of antiseptic surgery had crystallised in a hostile
recommendation; that one of Lister's patients had died;
and that the deceased's relatives had brought a suit for
negligence. What would have been the effect on surgery?
Where an auditor is faced with [such a] risk, the temptation
to play safe – by abandoning his independence of judgement
– is very great.[1]

Soon after qualifying as a chartered accountant I became convinced of the need for constant purchasing power accounting. My belief that accounts using money as the unit of measurement in a time of significant inflation could *never* give 'a true and fair view' meant there was no future for me in auditing, since I would never be able to sign an unqualified audit report!

Luckily there is no need for academics to allow official accounting standards to override their own judgement. They are still permitted, even encouraged, to think for themselves. What a pity that accountants and company directors no longer enjoy such a luxury. They have to follow orders. What happens if companies or their auditors disagree with the contents of accounting standards? They have to pretend to hold a view that in fact they do not.

The audit report on UK company accounts normally contains the following words: 'In our opinion the financial statements give a true and fair view of the state of affairs of the company and the group at the end of the financial year and of the group's profit and cash flows for the year then ended ...' But are the first three words correct? Are auditors still really giving their

---

1   W. T. Baxter, 'Recommendations on Accounting Theory', based on an article
    in *The Accountant*, 10 October 1953, reprinted in Baxter and Davidson, 2nd edn,
    op. cit., p. 424.

own opinion about the accounts giving 'a true and fair view'? Or are they now just certifying that they comply with accounting standards?

In the USA the SEC adds an important element of explicit compulsion. Its Accounting Series Release No. 4 (1938) stated that financial statements that are prepared in accordance with accounting principles for which there is 'no substantial authoritative support' will be presumed to be misleading or inaccurate. That must surely handicap new ideas! Indeed, 'the SEC's insistence on [this] ... has inhibited innovation in the past and could do so again'.[2]

In 1973 ASR No. 150 stated that: ' ... principles, standards and practices promulgated by the FASB will be considered by the Commission as having substantial authoritative support, and those contrary to such FASB promulgations will be considered to have no such support'. Such an authoritarian approach might not suit everyone. Suppose you sided with the minority in respect of an accounting standard involving a 4–3 decision. Your view would in effect be outlawed and there would be little chance of change to the standard for at least ten years.

The Chief Accountant of the SEC's Enforcement Division said in 1987: 'The essence of professionalism in accounting is the ability to exercise an independent judgement, even when that judgement runs counter to the client's wishes, and especially where the judgement cannot be supported by a clear statement in the literature.'[3] Fine words, but what about the requirement for 'substantial authoritative support'? In practice it hardly seems that the SEC

2   David Solomons, *Making Accounting Policy*, op. cit., p. 198.
3   R. J. Sack, quoted in Alister K. Mason, 'Professional judgement and professional standards', in Mumford and Peasnell, op. cit., p. 39.

encourages, or even permits, American accountants to exercise much personal judgement.

Several books[4] have listed dubious accounting practices such as various methods of inflating profits and off-balance-sheet finance to reduce apparent borrowings. As a result the term 'creative accounting' has become one of abuse, which is rather a pity. For there is plenty of need in accounting for creative thinking in dealing with new conditions, such as whether to discount liabilities or to capitalise finance leases. Accounting is an art not a science, and trying to outlaw thinking and imagination would cripple the profession. Restricting company accountants and auditors to checking compliance with rules is like requiring real artists, childlike, to paint by numbers.

Companies and auditors who claim to feel a need for precise rules, rather than the fuzzier 'spirit' of 'a true and fair view', become experts at hair-splitting. At the extreme such an approach implies that unless the rules explicitly prohibit it, anything goes. People search for loopholes and accounting starts to emulate tax legislation in its incomprehensible obscurity. Readers may recall Lord Diplock's sarcastic remark in the Court of Appeal: 'It would be a poor compliment to the draftsman of the 1960 Finance Act if this Court were to be unanimous as to its meaning.'[5] Could something similar be said of some accounting standards? We do need to remember that simplicity is a virtue, though it may now be too late for the ASB to adopt those words as its motto.

4   For example, Ian Griffiths, *Creative Accounting*, Firethorn Press, London, 1985; Michael Jameson, *A Practical Guide to Creative Accounting*, Kogan Page, London, 1988; Kamal L. Naser, *Creative Financial Accounting*, Prentice-Hall, Hemel Hempstead, 1993; Terry Smith, *Accounting for Growth*, Century Business, London, 2nd edn, 1996.

5   Diplock, LJ, IRC *v.* Parker, 1965.

Reducing competition in ideas and stopping evolution

Dearing criticised opinion-shopping: '… companies are increasingly prepared to challenge auditors, to shop for opinions, to seek counsel's opinion on the auditors' views and to change auditors'.[6] But why should the accounting profession resist competition in ideas? In some professions 'second opinions' can save lives: should we prohibit opinion-shopping among doctors or barristers?

The overriding requirement in the Companies Act is for accounts to give 'a true and fair view'. This clearly implies that *more than one* view may be 'true and fair', in which case what is wrong with consulting various accountants and comparing their (possibly different) opinions? A 'profession' surely involves some exercise of autonomous judgement, so it is hardly likely that everyone will agree on everything.

Teaching is probably as conservative a profession as accounting, mainly consisting of passing on received wisdom. But at least teachers pretend to encourage students to think for themselves, which it seems is no longer required of apprentice accountants. New accountants' education is incomplete unless they know more than just the current rules that standard-setters have imposed. How can they exercise independent judgement if they are unaware of the arguments against those rules, or even that there *are* any arguments against them? (During the debates about inflation accounting in the 1970s, many students just wanted to be told the 'official' answer.) Most accountants need to have some grasp of the history of their subject and how it has evolved. It would be a shame for accounting to suffer

6   Dearing, op. cit., p. 11.

from the same 'provincialism in time' of which Robbins[7] accused modern economics.

The process of preparing and exposing standards probably stimulates thinking and discussion about specific accounting topics. To that extent preparing standards may be a 'good thing'. But the act of issuing a mandatory standard may tend to stop or distort further evolution. Standard-setters should welcome unceasing debate as helping to lead towards better accounting. It may, however, sometimes be tempting for them to want to settle questions 'once and for all'. As Goodhart says: 'Novelty is a disturbing experience for the established, including the established authorities and regulators. It upsets the tidiness of life.'[8]

Indeed, practice may develop not as the result of rational human design but from spontaneous human action.[9] Thus[10] inadequate regulations attempted to steer financial accounting (in Germany) but triggered alternative readings of the rules and evasive action which frequently shifted practice in an unintended direction.

The ICAEW said in evidence to the 1926 Greene Committee: 'It is impossible by legislation to protect fools from their own folly.'[11]

---

7   Lionel Robbins, *The Theory of Economic Policy in English Classical Political Economy*, Macmillan, London, 1952, p. 2.

8   Charles Goodhart, 'The Costs of Regulation', in Arthur Seldon (ed.), *Financial Regulation – or Over-regulation?*, IEA, London, 1988, p. 25.

9   See F. A. Hayek, *Studies in Philosophy, Politics and Economics*, Routledge & Kegan Paul, London, 1967, ch. 6: 'The Results of Human Action but not of Human Design'.

10 Dieter Schneider, in Peter Walton (ed.), *European Financial Reporting*, Academic Press, London, 1995, p. 124.

11 Quoted in Lee and Parker, op. cit., p. 112.

Which recalls Herbert Spencer's remark: 'The ultimate result of shielding men from the effects of folly is to fill the world with fools.'[12]

Four important US accounting standards in the 1980s passed only by a bare 4–3 margin:

FAS 52: Foreign Currency Translation
FAS 87: Employers' Accounting for Pensions
FAS 89: Financial Reporting and Changing Prices
FAS 95: Statement of Cash Flows

One might expect many years to pass before the above standards were amended. FASB members might well be reluctant to reopen issues that caused severe problems in reaching a conclusion. But new FASB members might not agree with the members they replace on all these topics; or people who once opposed a standard may have changed their minds. Clearly the narrow balance of opinion may have shifted. It does seem an arbitrary way to set accounting rules, rather like musical chairs. Which accounting method can win the vote when the music stops? (There is no guarantee that the music will be played again for many years.) That is how the new International Accounting Standards Board will operate. One way to mitigate the problem is to require a 'super-majority'. As, for example, when the Marylebone Cricket Club proposed to change the rules to admit women members, a two-thirds majority was required on such an important matter.

In the UK there seem to have been only three dissensions

---

12   Herbert Spencer, 'State Tamperings with Money and Banks', in *Essays*, vol. iii, Macmillan, London, 1891, p. 354.

from twenty Financial Reporting Standards in ten years.[13] When there are clearly very serious disagreements between the ASB and 'ordinary' accountants, why don't ASB members disagree more among themselves? Even given the pressure for consensus such virtual unanimity on some very difficult questions seems remarkable. Or must potential ASB candidates sign up in blood to the Statement of Principles as a condition of entry? (As apparently IASB members must.)

In a voluntary regime people can continue to ponder tricky subjects and views can change slowly. For example, the UK permits both 'average rate' and 'closing rate' methods of translating profit and loss accounts from foreign currencies. The balance of practice has gradually been shifting towards the 'average rate' method. In 1982 two-thirds of those companies that disclosed a method favoured the 'closing rate' method, but ten years later three-quarters favoured the 'average rate' method. As long as a company is consistent, or clearly discloses if it changes its approach, does it matter that not all companies use the same method?

Those who think we should allow only one method have to decide which it should be. At one point the 'closing rate' method would probably have won the vote, whereas by 1992 the 'average rate' method was more popular. Thus a standard issued in 1982 might still be forcing UK companies to use the 'closing rate' method even though (as we know with hindsight) by 1992 a clear majority preferred the 'average rate' method. Do we really wish to force companies to continue using a method they have changed their minds about? Or is freedom to choose important? If so here, why not in respect of many other accounting topics too?

---

13   Messrs Bradfield, Main and Hinton in respect of FRS 3, 7 and 10 respectively.

Legitimising bad accounting

Gresham's Law, which states that bad money drives out good, assumes that the government interferes in the market by means of legal tender laws. In a free market for money good money would tend to drive out bad.[14] In the long run would good accounting in a free market likewise tend to drive out bad?

The sections of the early Companies Acts dealing with accounts tended to copy existing best practice. But where did 'best practice' come from in the absence of accounting standard-setters? Where will it come from in future? How fortunate that in those days we allowed commercial accounting to develop more or less freely.

Accounting standard-setting is to some extent a political process. On difficult questions a standard-setting body may be able to win the vote only through compromise. This may stem from business lobbying (as with goodwill in the UK) or from some government agency imposing the rules (as with railroad accounting in the USA) or from direct government interference (as with inflation accounting in both countries).

The existence of standards may legitimise bad accounting practices. Equally important it may *prohibit good accounting*. Examples of standards legitimising bad accounting are not hard to find. SSAP 13 requires companies to write off research as an expense even though it often creates an economic asset. SSAP 20 requires groups to use the closing-rate method to translate all balance sheet items even though the temporal method, which translates non-monetary assets at the historical exchange rate, better reflects the logic of group accounts. IAS 2 permitted the use of Last In First Out stock valuation (a US practice), which causes the balance

---

14   See Edwin Cannan, *An Economist's Protest*, P. S. King, London, 1927, p. 348.

sheet to undervalue stock and can lead to huge income statement distortions when out-of-date layers of LIFO stock are sold. SFAS 94 requires consolidation of all subsidiaries, even those in entirely different industrial sectors, so that the resulting aggregations are sometimes almost meaningless.

One of the most difficult topics has been goodwill, on which there has been intense lobbying (which UK standard-setters have found hard to resist) by companies wishing to avoid ever having to charge the cost of their acquisitions against profit. SSAP 22 *permitted* UK companies to treat purchased goodwill as a fixed asset and amortise its cost against profit over its useful life. This is the treatment I prefer, though guessing the length of life is often difficult and the best that can be done is consistent use of prudent estimates.

But nearly all UK companies followed SSAP 22's *preferred* treatment and deducted the cost of any purchased goodwill at once from reserves (shareholders' funds), even though that contravenes the detailed requirement in the Companies Act (see item 8 in Appendix 3). More importantly, that method overstates profit from the point of view of shareholders in the acquiring company. Post-acquisition group accounts include any profits from the acquired company but they only represent incremental 'profits' to the group after the total cost of acquiring them is charged as an expense.

Under stewardship accounting, it makes no sense for two successful companies to merge and for their new group accounts suddenly to disclose negative shareholders' funds. (This happened with SmithKline Beecham in 1989 and nearly with Glaxo Wellcome in 1995, when the group's book equity fell from over £5,000 million to less than £100 million.) At least SSAP 22 did not actually *require* bad accounting, it merely legitimised it. But many who favour standards dislike permitting any choice: they do not want competition or freedom or independent thinking.

The latest UK and US accounting standards on goodwill confuse the original cost of purchased goodwill with (an estimate of) its current value. By allowing companies to charge no expense against profit in respect of expiring purchased goodwill, if there is no evident 'impairment' of value, these standards permit companies in effect to capitalise internal spending on intangible assets 'by the back door'. There must be a risk that companies in trouble will tend to recognise 'impairment' (a subjective estimate) too late, though it is too early to have any evidence for this practice.

Unduly raising public expectations

Recent accounting scandals in the USA and elsewhere are said to have 'damaged confidence in the accuracy of company accounts', especially reported earnings. If so, that is indeed good news! People seem to expect far too much from accounts, hence reducing over-confidence may help to limit ultimate disappointment.

An 'intelligent public' should recognise a few basic points about accounting:

- It is very ambitious to aim to present the complex affairs of large companies in three summary financial statements, even with many pages of notes.
- In a going concern many transactions are incomplete at the balance-sheet date, and since many businesses own both partly produced goods and partly used-up assets the annual accounts have to contain estimates as to their future outcome.

- In making estimates about the uncertain future there are few uniquely 'correct' answers and competent people may honestly hold different views.
- Different companies, whether or not in the same industry, may quite properly use accounting policies which are not identical.

As the chairman of the Financial Reporting Review Panel remarked: 'The grey areas are a real problem. We are dealing with what are necessarily very sophisticated rules, designed to meet the needs of a huge variety of industries and commercial concerns. There is bound to be room for honest debate and difference of opinion.'[15]

It has been pointed out: 'Many aspects of business can't be quantified at all, e.g. employee morale, customer acceptance and management expertise. Many of those aspects which can be quantified do not permit precise measurement ... Even those aspects which do yield seemingly precise measures often yield different measures depending on the judgement of the measurer.'[16]

The first rule for company accounts should be: '*Caveat lector* – let the reader take care'. The accounting profession should not pander to ignorance by implicitly promising the public something it cannot deliver. Every company has its unique features and at best accounts can give only a very approximate impression of performance and financial position. There is bound to be a substantial 'margin of error' in accounts in a complex world, and we should not exaggerate their possible precision. A classic

---

15   Quoted in McBarnet and Whelan, op. cit., p. 65.

16   Shank, op. cit., p. 87.

American example is that of General Motors, which as recently as 1975 reported its results *to the nearest dollar:* yet I doubt that the accounts could have been accurate to better than the nearest 100 million dollars. (Did the SEC object to such spurious accuracy, one wonders?)

Standards cannot completely eliminate either fraud or error. Yet the existence of 'standards' tends to raise *beliefs* about the precision of company accounts above what is feasible, 'a climate of false security',[17] as it has been called. This is partly because of ballyhoo about what standards are attempting to do and partly because providing for enforcement implies (wrongly) that they can in fact do it. In that respect a much looser voluntary regime may actually do less damage.

The public cannot be experts on accounting, any more than on brain surgery or atomic physics (do we need official 'standards' in those fields too?). If the public expectations (or hopes?) are too high, then the accounting bodies and others should try to lower them to more sensible levels. Perhaps each set of accounts should carry a 'health warning' like a packet of cigarettes?[18] Education is no doubt important but it may not be the whole answer. Is it funny or sad that the Conference of Professors of Accounting still publishes its annual accounts as if they were accurate to the *nearest penny*!

That rather echoes the public's too-high expectation of accounts. It is ironic that at the same time the ASB appears to have too-*low* expectations of *accountants*. It leaves them little room for

---

17   F. L. Clarke, G. W. Dean and K. G. Oliver, *Corporate Collapse: Regulatory, Accounting and Ethical Failure,* Cambridge University Press, 1997, p. 37.
18   Richard Macve, *A Conceptual Framework for Financial Accounting and Reporting: Vision, Tool, or Threat?,* Garland Publishing, 1997, p. 99.

discretion on technical matters, overrides their obvious unhappiness with the 'new paradigm', and insists on telling them in ever more detail how to do their jobs. Indeed, this may lead to a vicious circle in which bright people are less and less willing to enter the accounting profession.

The present official approach proudly points to a distinguished Accounting Standards Board, appointed by a fairly representative Financial Reporting Council, an extensive consultation process, a Review Panel with powers to prosecute offenders, thirty accounting standards in issue, an Urgent Issues Task Force, which operates even more quickly than the ASB, etc., etc. The clear message is: '*You, the investing public, can safely rely on all this expert effort*'. But regulators sometimes seem to care more about being seen to attempt something than about actually achieving it. Meaning well is not the same as doing good.

6 GENERAL ACCEPTANCE?

It is highly desirable for both preparers and users of financial statements to understand and accept the rules of accounting. But the ASB is now basing its standards on principles that most accountants do not accept and on a model that seems irrelevant to most entities and users. The logical conclusion of the new revolutionary approach is to measure performance by deducting one volatile balance sheet from another, rather than by the traditional method of prudently matching expenses against earned revenues.

Accounting rules

Accounting does need rules. But Hayek[1] explained how rules can emerge and win general acceptance and perhaps change over time without any committee designing or imposing them. The very expression 'as a rule' implies there might be exceptions.

Ernst & Young's *UK & International GAAP*[2] distinguishes between 'generally accepted accounting *principles*' (the normal American term GAAP) and 'generally accepted accounting *practices*' (with the same GAAP acronym). It suggests that, in the UK,

---

1   F. A. Hayek, *Law, Legislation and Liberty*, Routledge & Kegan Paul, London, 1973, p. 11. See also his distinction (in ch. 2) between a *taxis*, or made order, and a *cosmos*, or spontaneous order.

2   Wilson et al., op. cit., p. 66.

'GAAP' refers to practices that *the accounting profession* regards as legitimate.

What is 'legitimate' according to Ernst & Young depends on the following:

- Do UK (or other) accounting standards permit the practice?
- Is it consistent with users' needs?
- Is it consistent with 'a true and fair view'?
- Do other companies in similar positions apply the same practice?
- Does the accounting literature provide support for it?

More than one accounting practice may be 'generally accepted' at any one time. If it were not so, how could accounting evolve? One would be in the hapless position of P. G. Wodehouse's would-be artist who can't paint any portraits until someone commissions him, yet nobody will commission him until he's painted some.

In 1971, SSAP 2 stated that four measurement principles (going concern; consistency from one year to the next; prudence; and the accruals concept) 'are practical rules rather than theoretical ideals'. They represent commercial wisdom and evolved as a result of more than a hundred years of practical experience. There was widespread agreement on such accounting principles long before SSAP 2 and then later the 1981 Companies Act required them. Only our modern standard-setters seem to dislike these principles; so much indeed that FRS 18 has now more or less abandoned prudence.

Both preparers and users of accounts need to understand the rules and accept them. The ASB's Statement of Principles says: 'Accounts will not be true and fair unless the information they contain is sufficient in quantity and quality to satisfy the reasonable expectations of the readers to whom they are addressed.'[3] In other words, we need to keep the content of accounts in line with the views of users, in order to avoid too large an 'expectations gap'.

Does it matter whether or not the *preparers* of accounts also 'accept' the accounting principles supporting the rules? In the long run the system seems unlikely to work if standard-setters in effect impose an alien creed on accountants. What sort of professionals will meekly accept orders they disagree with, about how to do their work?

If all you are doing is listing accounting principles that people already accept, why do you need *compulsory* accounting standards? But any body that intends to impose *revolutionary* changes does need a cloak of legitimacy. Watts and Zimmerman[4] claimed that the SEC's role was always to 'reform' existing accounting practice, hence it required 'accounting principles which do *not* describe existing practice'.

Before the Accounting Standards Board publishes a standard it issues an 'exposure draft' for comment. But the ASB need not abide by the majority view even if one is apparent. Many who agree with an exposure draft do not bother to respond, nor are all views of equal weight. So exposure for comment by no means makes standard-setting a democratic 'approval' process. It merely gives people a chance to express *disapproval*, which the ASB may then choose to ignore. (As the ASC did on Current Cost Accounting,

---

3   ASB, *Statement of Principles of Financial Reporting*, Introduction, para. 12.
4   Ross L. Watts and Jerold L. Zimmerman, 'The Demand for and Supply of Accounting Theories: The Market for Excuses', *Accounting Review*, April 1979, pp. 273–304.

.

which the members of the ICAEW explicitly voted against.[5]) With a government agency, the SEC, lurking in the background, the FASB in the USA cares even less about general acceptability than the ASB in the UK.

In fact the ASB sometimes gives the impression of a highly exclusive religious sect, vouchsafed a vision from heaven, whose destiny is to steer the benighted masses of old-fashioned accounting professionals towards the promised land, even against their own instincts. It has been suggested, by a strong supporter of the ASB, that 'financial statements prepared according to international standards will be unintelligible to all but a few'.[6] That is worrying. How can accounting practices be 'generally accepted' if hardly anyone understands them?

Why should everyone do the same?

Why should people want an Accounting Standards Board to dictate standards with which they disagree? Compulsory standards that really represent general agreement are hardly necessary, while those that don't are hardly desirable. The FASB compares accounting standards with traffic laws. It says that in the long run those who have to waive their personal preferences to observe common standards will gain more than they lose. (In the 1958 Swedish referendum on whether to switch from driving on the left to driving on the right, 85 per cent voted *not* to change, but they were overruled.) According to this expression of faith each company merely needs to understand correctly its own long-run interest.

---

5   See D. R. Myddelton, *On a Cloth Untrue: Inflation Accounting, the way forward*, Woodhead-Faulkner, Cambridge, 1984, p. 106.

6   David Damant, *Financial Times*, 6 June 2002.

But the analogy is false. Where there *needs* to be a single collective approach, as with traffic, most people are willing to accept one. There is no question of a 'personal preference'. Nobody cares *which* side of the road we drive on as long as, in any given area, we all do the same (for example, British drivers, used to driving on the left in their own country, have little trouble driving on the right on the continent of Europe). But one aspect of traffic laws may be relevant. In London new sets of traffic lights keep cropping up all over the place, yet they hardly ever seem to disappear. Are accounting standards like that, destined to proliferate until they cover the entire landscape?

A better analogy with accounting might be a smoking ban on trains even where some people want to be able to smoke. It would be absurd to claim that every single smoker 'gains' from such a ban. And in most cases there is no need for a complete ban. It is perfectly feasible to have 'smoking' compartments (clearly marked) at both ends of a train and 'non-smoking' ones in the middle. Then everyone knows where they are.

Does the desire for general acceptance mean that accounting standards allow too many alternatives? Solomons said: 'to be "generally accepted" is not the right test of the fitness of an accounting principle or procedure. The right test is whether it "tells it like it is"'.[7] But is there only *one* way to interpret the world? Perhaps 'general acceptance' may be a necessary, though not a sufficient, requirement for accounting principles.

If company directors (and auditors) think an accounting treatment in a specific case gives a true and fair view of financial posi-

---

7   David Solomons, *Guidelines for Financial Reporting Standards*, ICAEW, 1989, p. 8.

Table 1 **Ten possible accounting measurement choices**

1. Basis of measurement	Historical cost v. current value
2. Unit of account	Money v. unit of constant purchasing power
3. Nature of 'group'	Comprehensive v. some exclusions from consolidation

Various specific topics

4. Research & development	Expense as incurred v. some capitalisation
5. Stocks	Full costing v. marginal costing
6. Deferred tax	'Comprehensive' treatment v. 'flow-through' method
7. Pensions	Market valuations v. some 'smoothing' over time
8. Purchased goodwill	Test for impairment v. amortise over finite period
9. Executive stock options	Expense at time of grant v. do not expense
10. Foreign currencies	Closing-rate method v. temporal method

tion and performance, why should standard-setters forbid it? Who is likely to know best: the professionals on the ground close to real events or the 'experts' determined to impose a revolutionary set of principles which few practical accountants think make sense? There may be a case, however, for expecting companies to disclose clearly which treatment they have chosen.

Table 1 above lists ten possible choices on accounting measurement issues, all of which are mentioned in this paper. On most I happen to disagree with current mandatory accounting standards, but in any case it is the *compulsion* to which I object.

Balance sheet versus profit and loss account

Under the long-established 'matching' system ('transactions approach'), UK companies 'recognise' sales revenue when *earned* and charge expenses against it in the profit and loss account. There is currently no official UK accounting 'standard' on revenue recognition, though 'rules' have evolved over the years. This shows that we can sometimes do without 'standards' even in critical areas. But the balance sheet carries forward as 'assets' those costs that entities expect either to 'match' against *future* sales or to 'recover' out of ultimate sales proceeds. Thus the balance sheet is the link between 'going concern' profit and loss accounts.

Two major kinds of expenses in the profit and loss account are 'product' costs, directly matched against sales revenue, and 'period' costs. Companies normally write off, when incurred, so-called 'revenue investments' on research, advertising and training, because the possible future benefits are uncertain. They write off other expenses and losses if there is no reason to defer them.

One should distinguish matters of *timing* from more basic questions of measurement. For instance, the treatment of research and development expenditure or of deferred taxation affects the *period* in which accounts recognise income or expense. But some choices affect an enterprise's reported profit or loss over its *whole* lifetime: for example, whether to amortise goodwill, whether to expense executive stock options or whether to substitute constant purchasing power for money as the accounting unit of measurement.

There can be questions about which costs to match against sales. For instance, current accounting standards require the use of 'full costing', so that accounts treat some production overheads as potential 'cost of sales' and carry them forward as part of the 'cost' of closing stock. This treatment may allow a company to increase profits for a period by increasing production (and hence closing stocks and the proportion of total production overheads carried forward). An alternative would be to use 'marginal costing', expensing all overheads as 'period costs' and treating only direct costs as 'product costs'. Under the latter approach reported profits would vary more directly with sales revenue, which some people think makes more sense.

A key concept is 'prudence', in deciding when to recognise sales revenue, what provisions to make, and whether future sales revenues are sufficiently likely to justify carrying forward costs to match against them. Too much prudence might result in over-providing (and thus under-reporting profit) in one period, followed by writing back the over-provision (and thus over-reporting profit) in a subsequent period. This was the main objection to 'secret' reserves. On the other hand nearly everyone understood the system, and in general approved of the prudence concept ('don't count your chickens until they're hatched').

The scope for hidden discretion in applying judgement might lead to 'income smoothing' between periods. Revsine[8] suggested that managers and shareholders both like 'flexible' accounting practices: managers to help maximise bonus payments linked to periodic performance and shareholders to achieve more stable earnings. But while 'smoothing' is now out of fashion it does allow managements to give some emphasis to longer-term trends. This contrasts with the short-termism of annual accounts (and the even shorter-termism of quarterly reports).

For instance, a company's pensions liability under a defined benefit scheme is clearly long-term. In respect of a twenty-year-old employee it could stretch seventy years or more into the future. There is a case for 'smoothing' here, as everyone agreed until

---

8   Lawrence Revsine, 'The Selective Financial Misrepresentation Hypothesis', *Accounting Horizons*, December 1991, pp. 16–27.

recently. Using fleeting estimates of the marginal value of a few shares as the basis for valuing the whole of a company's equity capital is not beyond doubt. Nor is there agreement on which discount rate to use in valuing the liabilities.

The required FRS 17 accounting treatment seems to have led several companies to close down their 'defined benefit' schemes in order to avoid the possible resulting volatility in reported balance sheets and profit and loss accounts. In its 1995 Discussion Paper, the ASB opposed including pension assets and liabilities in the employer's accounts, on the various grounds that 'it would be a significant change from present accounting practice', 'including such amounts would not provide useful information' and 'current market prices may not be representative of the long-term expected outcome'.

Then, in its 1999 exposure draft FRED 20, the ASB changed its mind. It concluded that the UK should move into line with international practice and use 'market values' rather than actuarial values for scheme assets, 'as long as such an approach could be developed in a way that did not introduce undue volatility into the profit and loss account'. That may have seemed feasible as long as there was a separate Statement of Total Recognised Gains and Losses. But if this were now to be collapsed into a new 'comprehensive' income statement that objection again becomes critical.

So strong are the incentives for managers to avoid volatility in reporting results that preventing income-smoothing completely (if it were possible) might even tempt some companies to do things (to affect reported results) that they would not otherwise do. Income-smoothing might be less tempting if companies were still able to report 'extraordinary' items of profit or loss 'below the line' (as they could before FRS 3). Admittedly that system was open to abuse but it was transparent and readers were free to make appropriate adjustments as they saw fit.

Standard-setters around the world all broadly follow the FASB's conceptual framework. As a result they are now proposing a radical change to accounting by using a balance sheet approach. Instead of measuring profits by matching expenses against earned revenue, the new system would measure profits (or 'gains', as it calls them) by deducting one balance sheet's net assets from another's (after allowing for new capital, dividend payments, etc.). Thus the profit and loss account would become, in effect, the difference between two 'valuation' balance sheets.

The ASB defines 'the fair value of an asset' as 'the amount at which it could be exchanged in an arm's length transaction between informed and willing parties'. But there may often be a whole *range* of such values, not just one. The subjective process of valuation involves a hypothetical estimate which may be little more than a 'guess'. Hence there can be an enormous margin of error in trying to measure assets at 'fair values'. Indeed, many fixed assets may rarely be sold at all in the normal course of business except as part of a going concern or when worn out.

The balance sheet is a 'snapshot' at a moment in time. But in most ongoing businesses annual accounting bears no relation to the business cycle. Hence trying to establish reliable 'values' for second-hand specialised assets or for partly expired costs is very difficult. And it is almost impossible to measure the value of various intangible assets. So it seems reckless to try to deduce performance over a period from the difference between two highly unreliable net asset numbers. Reported profits under the new system would fluctuate far more from year to year, which would make it much harder than before to interpret short-term performance.

For example, suppose a company has paid no dividends and raised no new capital for two years, and that the book value of shareholders' funds (in £ million) was 1,000 at the end of Year 0, 1,100 at the end of Year 1, and 1,200 at the end of Year 2. On the face of it the company made a profit of £100 million in each of the two years. But if the margin of error in the balance sheet total each year was only 5 per cent, surely a very modest estimate, the possible variance in shareholders' funds and reported profits for the two years is as follows:

£ million	Shareholders' funds			Reported profit		
	Minimum	Central	Maximum	Minimum	Central	Maximum
Year 0	950	1,000	1,050			
Year 1	1,045	1,100	1,155	(5)	100	205
Year 2	1,140	1,200	1,260	(15)	100	215

Thus a margin of error in shareholders' funds as modest as 5 per cent can produce a range of possible variance of profits in the two years as follows:

(a) a loss of £5 million in Year 1 and a profit of £215 million in Year 2; or
(b) a profit of £205 million in Year 1 and a loss of £15 million in Year 2.

This is hardly satisfactory, yet it probably *understates* the possible variations.

Responses to the original Statement of Principles

Since 1990 the Accounting Standards Board has tried to develop a 'conceptual framework', laying down certain principles from which future standards could follow. To avoid alarming rank-and-file accountants they called it a 'Statement of Principles' (a 'less daunting phrase'[9]). Tweedie has said: '… not all standards will be based on the Statement of Principles. In some cases adherence to the Principles would result in too dramatic a change to be presently acceptable'.[10] That reveals the scale of the coming changes as well as acknowledging the need for an element of 'general acceptance'.

After several years' effort, in 1995 the ASB issued a draft Statement of Principles of Financial Reporting, which was not well received. The ASB claimed that critics misunderstood what it was saying, but it may be that most people understood only too well. In view of the hostile comments the ASB withdrew the draft in some disarray and a new version (not much changed) appeared after several more years in 1999.

Some of the comments from the (then) six[11] leading accountancy firms on the original draft Statement of Principles were devastating. Between them they audited the accounts of all the companies in the FTSE 100 and all but eight of the

---

9   Wilson et al, op. cit., p. 18.

10   David Tweedie, in Irvine Lapsley (ed.), *Essays in Accounting Thought: A Tribute to W. T. Baxter*, ICAS, 1996, p. 63.

11   The 'Big Eight' firms that dominated the profession from the 1960s to the late 1980s have subsequently become the 'Big Four': Arthur Andersen went out of business following Enron; Coopers & Lybrand merged with Price Waterhouse to become PricewaterhouseCoopers; Deloitte Haskins & Sells merged with Touche Ross to become Deloitte & Touche; Ernst & Whinney merged with Arthur Young to become Ernst & Young; Peat Marwick Mitchell became KPMG.

companies in the FTSE 250.[12] The comments can be summarised as follows:

Arthur Andersen[13]

- balance between stewardship and predictive value wrong;
- oppose split between P&L and STRGL;
- *support* greater use of current values;

Coopers & Lybrand[14]

- not enough emphasis on prudence, going concern and accruals;
- requirement for a 'true and fair view' should remain at the core of UK accounting;
- too much emphasis on unattainable 'predictive quality' from accounts;

Deloitte & Touche[15]

- ignores the legal context of accounts and a century of developed practice;
- not enough emphasis on the primary role of 'a true and fair view';
- excludes two fundamental accounting concepts: matching and going concern;

---

12 *Financial Times*, 6 January 2004.
13 Arthur Andersen, pp. 37–51 (of comments on the Statement of Principles).
14 Coopers & Lybrand, pp. 208–29.
15 Deloitte & Touche, pp. 248–55.

Ernst & Young[16]

- oppose proposal for asset/liability approach to supersede matching and prudence;
- oppose promotion of STRGL which diminishes P&L account;
- oppose phasing out historical cost in favour of current values;

KPMG[17]

- unhappy with emphasis on balance sheet rather than profit measurement;
- exaggerates the usefulness of accounts, with too much weight on predictive value;
- disagree with STRGL split from P&L;

Price Waterhouse[18]

- too much emphasis on predictive nature of accounts;
- generally *supportive* of current value;
- too much emphasis on balance sheet and assets/liabilities rather than profit measurement.

These views are summarised in Table 2, with obvious initials for the leading accountancy firms ('yes' and 'no' are self-explanatory; '(yes)' in brackets means relatively mild agreement or disagreement).

All six firms went out of their way to say they supported the ASB's initiative in trying to develop a Statement of Principles for

16 Ernst & Young, pp. 265–77.

17 KPMG, pp. 461–94.

18 Price Waterhouse, pp. 601–13.

Table 2 **Summary of comments from six leading firms**

	AA	DT	EY	KPMG	CL	PW
Too little emphasis on:						
'a true and fair view'	yes	yes	-	-	yes	yes
stewardship	yes	-	yes	yes	yes	(yes)
SSAP2 concepts	-	yes	yes	(yes)	yes	(yes)
legal context	-	yes	yes	yes	-	yes
Disagree with:						
asset/liability emphasis	(yes)	(yes)	yes	(yes)	-	yes
current values	no	(yes)	yes	(yes)	yes	no
STRGL versus P&L	yes	-	yes	yes	(yes)	-
predictive value focus	yes	-	yes	yes	yes	yes
opposed (out of 8)	4+(1)	3+(2)	7+(0)	4+(3)	5+(1)	4+(2)

Financial Reporting. But the detailed comments represented an overwhelming disagreement with the content of the draft Statement:

- a majority of the six firms disagreed with each one of the eight basic points above;
- each one of the six firms disagreed with a majority of the eight basic points.

Many of the firms' general assessments were very negative:

DT: '… we do not regard the draft as a sound basis for a final Statement';

EY: '… our overall view is that fundamental change to this draft is needed';

CL: '… we do not believe the ASB should move directly to a final version …';

PW: '… our reluctant conclusion is that the Board must start again!'

Clearly the ASB failed to gain 'general acceptance' for its 1995 Statement of Principles.

The revised Statement of Principles

The ASB issued a revised version of the Statement of Principles in 1999, but made few changes in response to all the critical comments. In the preface to the revised version the ASB said: 'The concerns raised about the draft's technical content have … been carefully considered and some changes have been made as a result.' But 'the main principles in this draft Statement are derived from an informal frame of reference the Board developed eight years ago to guide it in its work'. The message was clear: despite very serious dissent, especially from the six leading UK professional accountancy firms, the ASB had no intention of changing its mind.

The ASB's main opponents have not changed their mind either. Ernst & Young said: 'The new version of the *Statement of Principles* is no more convincing than its predecessor. … Since, by the ASB's own admission, the new version is little changed from its predecessor, the concerns that we raised in our 1996 submission remain valid, and *we append a copy of it* [emphasis added] rather than rehearsing these objections in detail once again.'[19] What a blistering response!

---

19   Ernst & Young, p. 80 (of comments on the Revised Statement of Principles).

As a result of the comments on the 1995 version of the Statement of Principles, the ASB does appear to have backed away somewhat from current values for the time being and to be rethinking the STRGL. But there is no change to the emphasis on the balance sheet and assets and liabilities versus the matching concept and the profit and loss account.

For example, the ASB defines liabilities as 'obligations of an entity to transfer economic benefits as a result of past transactions or events'. Thus if someone buying a magazine pays a year's subscription in advance the publisher has a 'liability' to provide the agreed number of issues over the next year. Under the matching system the publisher would normally recognise profit (that is, revenue and cost) on a pro rata basis, in effect matching average cost against revenue month by month. But the 'current value' approach could argue that the publisher ought to value its 'liability' only at *marginal* cost since that is the economic cost of settling it. This would imply recognising nearly all the expected ultimate profit as soon as the sale occurred. In practice this is not (yet) done. So the ASB is fudging its principles, just as in the bad old days before we had a conceptual framework to ignore when expedient.

Moreover, there are problems in valuing a company's debt obligations at current values. It seems pointless since nearly all of them will ultimately be settled at par value; and using a company-specific discount rate means that the poorer a company's credit rating the lower the 'value' of its debt.

The ASB now uses the term 'investor' to mean both existing and potential investors. This represents an important divergence from UK company law. Even if the Statement of Principles, aiming at potential investors, were suitable for the accounts of publicly listed companies, it seems totally inappropriate for small family-owned private companies and all the other not-for-profit entities. They hardly care at all about potential investors.

So the ASB seems to be basing its accounting standards on a conceptual framework that is totally irrelevant for the vast majority of entities producing accounts, and on principles that most professional accountants do not accept. A non-problem followed by a non-solution! Perhaps that sums up the history of accounting standards.

7 POLITICAL INTERFERENCE

Those aspects of company law that affect accounts clearly stem from government. But accounting standards too, even when seemingly produced by professional accounting bodies or 'independent' boards, may be subject to 'political' (i.e. 'government') interference. Several examples are a matter of public record, but many others may have occurred behind the scenes. Perhaps the most notorious political interference concerned inflation accounting in the 1970s, both in the UK and in the USA. Even potential intervention can have a significant impact, as with the EU's threat not to endorse future international accounting standards. Since accounting scandals, like the poor, are always with us, knee-jerk government reactions such as the Sarbanes-Oxley Act in the USA are unlikely to be appropriate.

Political interference in the United Kingdom

Chapter 2 noted the voluntary nature of company accounts for nearly half a century between 1856 and 1900. Nowadays, in contrast, there is extensive government involvement in many aspects of our economic life. In fact since World War II deliberate action by British governments has caused far more serious damage to investors than any absence of accounting standards ever could have done. As the following examples illustrate, it might be naive to suppose that governments attach importance to protecting investors.

For many years UK law required trustees to invest in government securities a large part of the funds under their control (the Chinese government recently issued a similar edict). This purported to limit risk but in fact only ensured heavy losses. Between 1946 and 1961, when the Trustee Investment Act relaxed the rules, the real value of long-term British government stock fell by about 72 per cent[1] (as interest rates rose to allow for the inflation that also destroyed the real value of long-term government stock).

Foreign exchange controls were introduced in 1939 as a 'temporary' measure on the outbreak of war, yet they lingered on for a third of a century after the end of World War II. These controls trapped British residents until 1979, causing them huge post-war losses as the pound sterling declined by 50 per cent against the US dollar and by no less than 80 per cent against the Swiss franc.

Above all the British tax system has crushed UK investors.[2] If we look at total taxes as a percentage of national income, the twentieth century saw an increase in the UK from 10 per cent in 1900 (unusually *high* owing to the Boer War!) to more than 40 per cent in 2000. Just as company accounts cannot quantify everything of importance in business, so too that tax ratio does not reveal the full extent of state control of prices, regulations, etc. But it gives

1	Price of 2.5% Consols (avg):	1946: 96.3;	1961: 46.1
	£'s purchasing power (1900 = 100):	1946: 32.9;	1961: 19.2
	Real '1900' price of 2.5% Consols:	1946: 31.7;	1961: 8.9

Loss of purchasing power 1946–61 = 72%.

Source: David and Gareth Butler, *British Political Facts 1900–1985*, Macmillan, London, 1986, pp. 380–1.

2   D. R. Myddelton, *The Power to Destroy: A study of the British tax system*, Society for Individual Freedom, London, 2nd edn, 1994.

the proper flavour of a massive increase in government interference.

For forty years up to 1979 the top rate of UK tax on income from investments exceeded 90 per cent. This may be hard for younger readers to believe. These penal rates of confiscation, which all political parties supported, raised very little if any net revenue for the government. Their purpose was to hurt the rich, not to help the poor. And capital 'gains' tax, whose net yield was also very small, if not actually negative, failed to allow for currency debasement between 1965 and 1982; it thus taxed people on overstated or non-existent real gains. During this period the pound lost over 80 per cent of its purchasing power.

Chapter 2 outlined key provisions of various Companies Acts between 1844 and 1989. According to Benston,[3] the Conservative government's fall early in 1974 averted one potential piece of highly interventionist legislation. Clause 69 of the lapsed Companies Bill would have empowered the Secretary of State for Trade and Industry '… to prescribe by regulations the matters to be disclosed in accounts, directors' and auditors' reports and annual returns and to make different provisions for different classes of companies'. The same secretary of state, Peter Walker, did in fact intervene in one key area: inflation accounting.

Inflation accounting in the United Kingdom: a case study

The UK debate over inflation accounting between 1973 and 1985 illustrates the nature and effect of government intervention

---

3   Benston, *Corporate financial disclosure*, op. cit., pp. 2–3.

in accounting. It is worth briefly telling the story as a dreadful warning of what not to do.

The foundations of British accounting were laid in the eighteenth and nineteenth centuries. In those days, for practical purposes, the value of money was stable. As far as one can tell[4] the general level of prices was about the same on the outbreak of World War I in 1914 as it had been on the restoration of Charles II in 1660. Between those dates, except only during the Napoleonic Wars and their aftermath, the annual rate of change in the general price level never averaged more than 2 per cent over any fifteen-year period. Hayek[5] taught his German students what price stability meant by producing in a 1963 lecture a British penny dated 1863 which he had recently received in change. It was still in circulation after a hundred years.

But things changed after World War II. The pound's purchasing power halved in the twenty years between 1945 and 1965, halved again between 1965 and 1975, and halved *again* between 1975 and 1980. Accounting in terms of the British monetary unit no longer meant accounting in terms of (roughly) constant purchasing power. In the fifteen years between 1965 and 1980 the pound lost no less than three-quarters of its purchasing power (other currencies too suffered rapid inflation). It is hardly surprising that a rate of currency debasement unprecedented in sterling's thousand-year history should cause problems for UK accounting.

---

4   Phyllis Deane and W. A. Cole, *British Economic Growth 1688–1959*, Cambridge University Press, 2nd ed., 1967, pp. 17–18 and Fig. 7 pull-out at end.

5   F. A. Hayek, *New Studies in Philosophy, Politics, Economics and the History of Ideas*, Routledge & Kegan Paul, London, 1978, pp. 221–2.

Constant purchasing power accounting

My own first article urging 'inflation accounting' appeared in December 1965.[6] In August 1968 the ICAEW published a pamphlet showing how to adjust accounts to allow for inflation. Clearly on this sensitive topic it would be both important and difficult to get agreement on any specific proposal. But at this stage the UK government said[7] it preferred to leave the problem of inflation accounting to the profession to solve.

The logic of inflation accounting (Constant Purchasing Power (CPP) accounting) is simple. When the purchasing power of money is changing over time accounts should treat money amounts at different points in time as if they were 'foreign' currencies. For purposes of translation CPP accounting uses the Retail Prices Index as an 'exchange rate' over time,[8] as a (reciprocal) measure of the 'general purchasing power of money'.

If you buy something for £100 and sell it for $150 you have not made a 'profit' of $50. Nobody suggests deducting pounds from dollars. Similarly, if you buy something for $_{87}$£100 and sell it for $_{04}$£150 you have not made a 'profit' of $_{04}$£50. (Since $_{87}$£100 is equivalent in purchasing power to $_{04}$£185 you have in fact made a *loss* of $_{04}$£35 in 'real terms' or constant purchasing power terms.) But some people (including the ASB) do suggest that you have made a profit.

When the value of money is stable, money itself is a unit of constant purchasing power. But if the value of money is not stable over time then people care more about purchasing power: children

6   D. R. Myddelton, 'Inflation and Accounts', *Accountancy*, December 1965.

7   D. S. Morpeth, 'Developing a Current Cost Accounting Standard', in Ronald Leach and Edward Stamp (eds), *British Accounting Standards: The First 10 Years*, Woodhead-Faulkner, Cambridge, 1981, p. 44.

8   See the first sentence of L. P. Hartley, *The Go-Between*, Hamish Hamilton, 1953: 'The past is a foreign country: they do things differently there.'

and their pocket money, workers and their wages, pensioners, house-owners, users of accounts. Hence the widespread use of index-linking. In times of inflation all sensible comparisons of financial amounts over time have to be made, perhaps implicitly, in terms of constant purchasing power. CPP accounting does this explicitly.[9]

In August 1971 the ASSC published a Discussion Paper on Inflation and Accounts. In January 1973, after extensive consultation, and with the agreement of the Confederation of British Industry, the ASSC published Exposure Draft (ED) 8, proposing Current Purchasing Power accounting (which I prefer to call Constant Purchasing Power accounting). The government disliked it and in July 1973, six months later, announced it would set up a committee to look into the problem, with Francis Sandilands as chairman. Few governments bother to set up committees if they agree with what is being proposed. The government's terms of reference emphasised relative price changes as well as general inflation, a hint that Mr Sandilands (later Sir Francis Sandilands) and his committee picked up.

After six more months of raging inflation, the government finally announced the names of the dozen members of the Sandilands Committee. Two of the three accountants had no special interest in the subject: in order to derive a 'fresh and uncommitted view', the committee was to exclude any accountants who had publicly discussed the subject. The third accountant member, though, was Michael Inwards,[10] who was known to be a keen supporter of replacement cost accounting. Thus the

---

9   For a fuller account, see Myddelton, *On a Cloth Untrue*, op. cit.

10   He worked for Pye of Cambridge, a subsidiary of Philips Lamps, the Dutch multi-national that used and proselytised for replacement cost accounting.

committee membership would appear to have been biased from the start.

Only three members were accountants. As Stamp said:

> [A]ccounting standards … cannot be left to amateurs … If the constructors who constructed a fine hotel had entrusted the installation of its electrical system to a gang of twelve people composed of three electricians, six company directors, an economist, a lady, and the ex-Secretary General of the TUC, it would not surprise me if the management received a shock when they turned the lights on.[11]

In the event the Sandilands Committee rejected CPP and proposed a form of replacement cost accounting called Current Cost Accounting (CCA) that completely ignored general inflation. This was somewhat surprising in that between July 1973 and September 1975, when the Committee published its report, the Retail Prices Index had risen by 50 per cent.

The Sandilands Report's anti-CPP arguments were very thin. One might have expected a lengthy discussion about whether or not money was still a suitable unit of account (the Retail Prices Index rose by more than 25 per cent in the year to September 1975). Instead all we got, in para. 204, was a single sentence of flat assertion: 'The pound is equally useful as a unit of measurement to all users of published accounts and to all individuals and entities in the economy.' Para. 414 even argued that the constant purchasing power unit would 'not have a constant value in terms of the monetary unit' – an astonishing comment from the self-styled Inflation Accounting Committee. How anyone in the mid-1970s in England could regard the monetary unit as a paragon of constancy

---

11　E. Stamp, as quoted in Mumford and Peasnell, op. cit., p. 33.

against which to measure the unreliability of other potential units of account is something of a mystery.

The government demanded a response from the accounting bodies within just over two months. This was not long to consider a CCA system completely different from the CPP system that the accountants themselves had proposed. We shall never know what would have happened if the professionals had rejected the Sandilands CCA proposals outright. That is hypothetical, like the whole CCA system. Clearly it would have been awkward for the government, but it might have been good for accounting and for the independence of the profession. British governments should not have interfered in inflation accounting but British accountants should not have let them.

Current Cost Accounting standard

In the event the government then instructed the ASC to produce an accounting standard based on CCA. Over the next ten years the government kept on saying: 'Implement a form of CCA.' It never invited the profession in the light of the Sandilands Report to choose the best of the rival methods. This was not an accounting choice but a political one.

In due course the Guidance Manual to ED 18, the CCA exposure draft, appeared. It was more than four hundred pages long. In 1977 the members of the ICAEW passed a unique resolution saying they did not wish any system of Current Cost Accounting to be compulsory, but their views were ignored. The question of 'general acceptability' no longer applied, and over the next few years a series of CCA proposals appeared. ED 18 was abandoned owing to complexity; the Hyde Guidelines were only a stopgap;

and ED 24, a revised exposure draft, led after further changes to SSAP 16, which finally appeared in 1980.

The CCA standard SSAP 16 was needlessly complex and technically flawed (for instance, depreciation expense was in end-of-year pounds, while other expenses were in average-for-the-year pounds). Many companies soon simply ignored it, with the connivance of their auditors, even though it was supposed to be mandatory (as CPP never was). Thus, although the government appeared to have the power to enforce its preferred approach to inflation accounting, in the event this proved to be an illusion.

Conclusion

At the end of a decade of rapid UK inflation there was less agreement on inflation accounting than there had been at the beginning. The politicians of both main parties helped to bring into disrepute the whole process of private sector accounting standard-setting. As so often when we seem to see a spotlight on 'market failure', behind the scenes the real villain is interference by government. Indeed, it was fear of precisely this which induced the accountants to start issuing 'standards' (rather than merely recommendations) in the first place.

The main good that resulted, though at a high cost indeed, was a stronger than ever repugnance towards political interference in accounting. But some elder statesmen remained steadfast in their view that politicians rather than accountants knew best. At the 1983 Annual Conference of the ICAEW, a guest speaker attacked the accounting profession for not solving the problem of accounting for inflation. Who was it? None other than Edward

Heath, prime minister in the government that had sabotaged the accountants' own CPP proposal.

Political interference in the United States

There are several examples of political interference in accounting in the USA, where the SEC, a government agency, has been prominent since 1934. According to Spacek,[12] the Interstate Commerce Commission, a US government agency, permitted railroads 'to issue financial statements with woefully inadequate depreciation provisions and reserves – something that no other business would dare do. But the Commission rules furnish the authority that enables the public accountant to ignore his professional responsibility in expressing his opinion on the railroad statements'.

Likewise May[13] noted that US agencies had acquired jurisdiction over accounting matters with adverse results: 'the practices which had become discredited were more general in the regulated industries ... '

'In America, one important experiment was stopped because it offended "accepted accounting principles"... The SEC compelled the US Steel Company to amend 1947 depreciation figures based on the current price level, and so prevented all further experiment in this field by companies under SEC control.'[14] And the SEC for a long time refused to file accounts drawn up in vertical form.[15]

---

12 Leonard Spacek, address at the Harvard Business School, September 1959, reprinted in Sidney Davidson et al. (eds), *An Income Approach to Accounting Theory*, Prentice-Hall, Englewood Cliffs, NJ, 1964.

13 May, *Financial Accounting*, op. cit., p. 258.

14 Baxter, op. cit., 2nd edn, p. 423.

15 R. C. Morris, *Corporate Reporting Standards and the 4th Directive*, Research Committee Occasional Paper, ICAEW, 1975, p. 31.

In 1962 the SEC contradicted the APB's Opinion No. 2 requiring the investment tax credit to be accounted for by the deferment method. A similar thing happened in 1971 on the same subject, but this time involving Congress. In 1976 the SEC's requirement for replacement cost information effectively sabotaged the FASB's preference for constant dollar accounting (in the same way as the British government sabotaged the ASSC's preference for CPP accounting). In 1978 the SEC overturned the FASB's attempt (in SFAS 19) to standardise oil and gas accounting.

More recently, in the early 1990s political pressure and intensive lobbying defeated the FASB's proposal to expense executive stock options. Later, post-Enron, politicians complained that companies were over-stating profits, even though this was partly due to their own meddling.

In 2000 the chairman of a Senate committee objected to the FASB's proposal to require amortisation of goodwill and proposed instead a periodic impairment test. Within a few months the FASB rushed out a revised exposure draft reversing its earlier proposals.[16]

In addition to these instances of political interference there are many other examples of industry lobbying on accounting matters.[17]

Political interference in the European Union

Chapter 3 described how the accounting approach of many contin-

---

16 Stephen A. Zeff, 'Political Lobbying on Proposed Standards', *Accounting Horizons*, 16(1), March 2002, p. 51.

17 See Stephen A. Zeff, 'The Rise of "Economic Consequences"', *Journal of Accountancy*, December 1978.

ental European countries depended largely on government action, unlike the traditionally more laissez-faire attitude of the British authorities. The European Union's Company Law Directives have covered a good deal more than just accounting; but the Fourth and Seventh Directives certainly affected UK accounting, *inter alia* by setting out required formats for balance sheets and profit and loss accounts as well as by prescribing measurement methods.

It is also worth noting that while the EU is requiring listed companies to comply with IASB standards from 2005, the Commission has reserved the right, if it sees fit, *not* to endorse certain standards in future. Any such failure to endorse an international standard would itself amount to political interference. The French president has publicly complained about certain aspects of the proposed international accounting standard on derivatives. And recently the EU commissioner responsible for accounting suggested[18] that, failing agreement with the banks, the IASB should abandon disputed sections of IAS 39, otherwise the Commission could find it 'difficult' to approve it.

Accounting scandals

The stimulus for ad hoc accounting regulation has often been so-called 'scandals', which governments and others are unwilling to seem to tolerate. But this *political* reaction may overrate our power to prevent them. Galbraith's theory[19] of the 'bezzle' (the stock at any time of undiscovered embezzlement) suggests it goes up in booms and shrinks again in busts. From time to time accounting

---

18   Frits Bolkestein and his spokesman, *Financial Times*, 24 January 2004.

19   J. K. Galbraith, *The Great Crash*, Penguin, 1954, pp. 152–3.

Table 3 **Accounting scandals**

Adecco	Dynegy	Minsec
Adelaide Steamship	Eastern Counties Railway	National Student
Adelphia	El Paso	Marketing
Communications	Enron	Nortel
Ahold	Equity Funding	Nvidia
Albert Fisher	European Commission	Oxford Health Plans
Alstom	Four Seasons Nursing	Parmalet
AOL/Time Warner	GEC/AEI	Penn Central
Argyll Foods	Global Crossing	Pergamon Press
Ashtead	Gollins Holdings	Polly Peck
Associated British Ports	Grand Metropolitan	Poseidon
Atlantic Computers	Green Department Store	Quality Software Products
Barchris Construction	Green Tree Financial	Queens Moat Houses
Barlow Clowes	Halliburton	Qwest
BCCI	HealthSouth	Rank Hovis McDougall
Bond Corporation	HIH	Reid Murray
Holdings	Home Stake Production	Rite Aid
Brent Walker	IBM	Rolls Razor
Brentford Nylons	ImClone Systems	Rolls-Royce
Britannia Securities	Insull Utility Investment	Royal British Bank
British & Commonwealth	Int'l Signals and Control	Royal Mail Steamship
British Aerospace	Interpublic	Rush & Tomkins
British Airways Authority	Interstate Hosiery Mills	Saatchi & Saatchi
British Printing	Investors Overseas	Skandia
BTR	Services	Spring Ram
Burton Group	Kreditanstalt	Storehouse
Cendant	Kreuger & Toll	Sunbeam
Cisco	Ladbroke Group	Swedish Match
City Equitable Fire	Leasco	Texas Gulf Sulphur
Insurance	Lemont & Hauspit	Tiphook
City of Glasgow Banking	Levitt Group	Trafalgar House
Coloroll	Lockheed	Tyco International
Computer Associates	London & County	US Realty & Construction
Conseco	Securities	Vehicle & General
Consolidated Cotton	London Capital Group	Versailles
Duck	Lonrho	Waste Management
Continental Vending	Lucent	Worldcom
Corporate Services Group	Maxwell Communications	WPP
Court Line	McKesson & Robbins	Xerox
Courtaulds	Micro Focus	Yale Express
Cray Electronics	Microstrategy	Yale Transport

scandals are bound to arise, whether we have 'accounting stand-ards' or not. (Of course, we cannot tell how many problems the existence of accounting standards may have helped to *prevent*. But were there really so many more or worse accounting scandals in the days before we had any 'standards'?)

H. L. Mencken[20] wrote a piece lamenting the death of a long list of gods, once thought immortal, whose name nobody today even remembers. On a more mundane level, Table 3 lists well over one hundred names of companies once involved in accounting scandals, many of which most of us have now almost completely forgotten. I define 'scandal' here as something causing public outrage or controversy, but it must be stressed that there is no implication of fraud. Very few of the people running the companies listed opposite were charged with any offence, and of those that were several were acquitted. Some of the 'scandals' merely reflect public ignorance about accounting.

I have not tried to analyse the cases by date or country. Being most familiar with the UK and the USA, no doubt I have missed out many worthy candidates from other parts of the world. And only very striking events from before World War II are likely to have come to my attention. It is worth noting that most of the scandals above occurred *after* the introduction of accounting standards.

The point is that scandals are a constant. So governments should think carefully before using accounting scandals as a reason or excuse for further interference in company reporting require-ments. Knee-jerk responses such as the Sarbanes-Oxley Act in the USA are unlikely to be appropriate.

---

20 H. L. Mencken: 'Memorial Service', in *Prejudices, Third Series 1922*, reprinted in 'A Mencken Chrestomathy', Knopf, New York, 1967, pp. 95–8.

8 SETTING AND ENFORCING STANDARDS

This chapter discusses who should set and enforce accounting standards and considers the costs of standards. In earlier chapters we have discussed some of the problems with accounting standards where discretion is removed from individual professionals. In Chapter 7 we saw how political interference in the process of standard-setting can make matters worse. That still leaves an open question. What bodies should be involved with standard-setting and to what extent? Even if rigid standard-setting by professions and private organisations is bad practice there is still a difference between competing professional organisations, competing stock exchanges, and so on, developing their own accounting and reporting standards, and compulsory standard-setting by governments: although from a legal point of view there is probably little difference between the authority of public and private standard-setters.

There appear to be four main contenders for the task of setting accounting standards: professional accounting bodies, stock exchanges, representative boards, and government agencies. The distinction between the private sector and the public sector seems relatively unimportant. The critical question is how the courts (ultimately) could judge whether a company's accounts meet the legal requirement to give 'a true and fair view'.

The total direct costs of setting and enforcing accounting standards do not seem high compared with the annual cost of auditing company accounts. But they are probably much outweighed by all the indirect costs, which are not easy to measure.

Accounting regulation

Accounting standard-setting bodies have many tasks. They need to:

- decide which items to place on their agenda;
- formulate an approach to specific topics;
- expose drafts for public comment and amend them in the light of public reaction;
- issue final proposals as 'standards';
- keep in touch with what standard-setters in other countries are up to; and
- keep topics under review from time to time.

There are at least four different kinds of shareholders, whose needs with respect to company accounts may differ:

- sophisticated large investors in listed companies, such as fund managers and analysts;
- small investors in listed companies;
- controlling investors in unlisted 'family' companies;
- other smaller investors in unlisted companies.

Accounting standards are currently intended mainly for large companies and large investors in them. It seems highly doubtful that accounting standards are relevant for small companies.

Beresford[1] has summarised the arguments for private versus public responsibility for setting accounting standards. The private sector has greater expertise and practical experience, and is more likely to produce standards consistent with a set of agreed underlying concepts, but it may be subject to conflicts of interest. The public sector will be more concerned with 'economic consequences' and more subject to special-interest lobbying, but may be likely to do a better job of cost–benefit analysis. But Cairns[2] points out that the IASC does not distinguish between private sector and government standard-setting bodies.

Table 4[3] shows potential private and public UK standard-setters from left to right.

A regime's status may not always be entirely clear. For example, between 1945 and 1990 the accounting profession's pronouncements moved from 'voluntary' to 'compulsory'. The ICAEW's Recommendations between 1945 and 1969 were clearly 'voluntary', while from 1970 to 1990 companies (and their auditors) were 'expected' to follow Statements of Standard Accounting Practice. Even though the ASC's enforcement procedures may to some extent have 'lacked teeth', accountants could at least in theory have been expelled from their professional bodies for failing to follow them.

Similarly it could be argued that the Financial Research Council, which appoints the members of the Accounting Standards Board in the post-1990 regime, is independent of government. Yet the government appoints the chairman and three deputy chairmen

---

1   Dennis R. Beresford, *Accounting Horizons*, June 1995.
2   David Cairns, 'The Future Shape of Harmonization: a reply', *European Accounting Review*, 6(2), 1997, p. 332.
3   Freely adapted from Flower and Ebbers, op. cit., p. 104.

Table 4 **Possible standard-setting bodies**

Public or private body?	Type of body	Examples	Forms of regulation issued and enforced
Private	Accountancy profession	CCAB	Recommendations or standards
Private	Stock exchange*	LSE	Trading rules
Public	Representative board	Financial Reporting Council**	Accounting standards
Public	Government	EC, UK government	Companies Acts, European Directives

* Many of the functions and requirements of stock exchanges have been taken over by a public body, the FSA. European Union legislation is increasingly encroaching on aspects of private regulation that have been developed traditionally by stock exchanges.
** Appoints and funds ASB and FRRP.

as well as two other persons, and the chairman and deputy chairmen then nominate the other twenty or so members. That is not what one would normally understand by 'independence'.

The position with respect to enforcement is somewhat mixed. Even though professional accountancy bodies themselves might not be able or willing to 'enforce' their own standards, stock exchanges could *require* listed companies to follow them, and courts could 'normally expect' all companies to do so. In addition, most people would regard representative boards and governments as politically legitimate. Thus a representative board, seeking to enforce the government's (Companies Act) requirement for accounts to give 'a true and fair view', might ask a court to hold that accounts failing to follow an accountancy body's 'voluntary' standard resulted in not giving 'a true and fair view'.

Professional accounting bodies

Most preparers of company accounts and all auditors are account-ants by profession, as are many who 'use' accounts. For views about medicine one goes to doctors and for views about buildings to architects or surveyors, so for views about accounts it seems sensible to go to accountants. Nearly all the members of the ASB, FASB and IASB are accountants.

Each professional accounting body could choose to issue its own technical guidelines to its own members. The various bodies would agree on some topics, perhaps on many, but probably not on all. Indeed, such competition might be healthy in preventing guidelines from carrying too much 'authority'. It would keep the way open for practice to evolve. It would also emphasise the personal and collective responsibility of direc-tors for company accounts and of auditors for their opinions on them.

In due course the number of different accounting practices in some areas would probably decline, while in others it might even increase for a time. Permitting some choice if there are several views may turn out to improve accounting more than trying to suppress dissent.

Members would of course be perfectly free to ignore guidelines from their own professional body. So in order to be useful the stand-ards would depend on general acceptance. No doubt accounting bodies would consult their members widely before issuing guide-lines, as they always did in the past, with Recommendations as well as with Standards.

There may be little point in aiming for a more 'representative' body to issue voluntary guidelines. This aspect relates less to the quality of any 'standards' than to the need for political legitimacy[4] to allow *enforcement*. Although in theory professional bodies could threaten to expel members who failed to comply even with 'mandatory' standards, in practice they are very reluctant to do so (in law and medicine as much as in accounting).

The International Accounting Standards Board, which cannot itself enforce its standards, could become the International Accounting Suggestions Board on behalf of professional accountancy bodies around the world. A voluntary approach might reduce the existing pressure for imperfect compromises.

Stock exchanges

Stock exchanges are clearly not the proper bodies to establish general accounting practice, since the vast majority of companies that need accounts are small and unlisted and have nothing to do with the stock exchange. In addition, there are large numbers of not-for-profit organisations that need accounts. Hence, incidentally, the SEC too should have only a limited role to play in accounting standard-setting.

Neither the Companies Act nor any UK accounting standard requires companies to publish interim accounts more frequently than once a year (in a sense even annual accounts are only 'interim' for a going concern). The requirement to publish accounts more frequently than once per year is one of the few remaining UK accounting requirements that originated from the stock exchange. Another is the requirement for companies to publish ten-year summaries of the profit and loss account.

---

4   Michael Bromwich stresses this point in *The Economics of Accounting Standard Setting*, Prentice-Hall/ICAEW, London, 1985.

The market might value extra details in respect of certain industries, for example gold mining, oil exploration or pharmaceuticals; but companies could remain free to supply them or not as they chose. The incentive would be a potentially higher share price, due to a lower cost of capital, and/or a better credit rating. This voluntary approach, in my view, could be greatly extended.

Even very large companies have not always thought an audit essential. Alfred P. Sloan reports[5] in 1919 advising Mr Durant, the founder of General Motors, that he thought the corporation should have an independent audit in view of the large public interest in its shares. GM's sales in that year were over $500 million (equivalent very roughly to $5,000 million today). But this example does show that some companies at least chose to have their accounts audited even though they were not obliged to do so. The same applies today to many non-listed US companies, which are not required to have their accounts audited, as well as to many partnerships.

Stock exchanges possess enforcement powers in that they can refuse to list the shares of companies that fail to follow suitable accounting standards. The London Stock Exchange (LSE), now under the aegis of the Financial Services Authority (FSA), requires UK companies to follow ASB accounting standards but permits foreign companies to use IAS or to follow local laws.

It seems healthy for stock exchanges to *compete* with each other. If the New York Stock Exchange, for example, requires foreign companies listing their shares to comply with US GAAP, then the market can determine whether the SEC's requirements are worthwhile. If not – if the costs exceed the perceived benefits – other stock

---

5   Alfred P. Sloan, *My Years with General Motors*, Penguin, Harmondsworth, 1986, p. 25.

exchanges may gain business as a result. That is Hayek's competition as a 'discovery procedure' at work.[6] In contrast, current discussion between the IASB and IOSCO concerning agreement on compulsory worldwide standards for listed companies represents a more authoritarian approach aiming at global monopoly.

Representative boards

In recent years a view has emerged that standard-setting bodies (or at least the group that appoints the standard-setters) ought to include users of accounts as well as preparers and auditors. Hence after 1996 the IASC co-opted representative bodies in an attempt to make their standards more acceptable. Even so there often appears to be no more than a single token 'user' on standard-setting boards. Nearly all the places are reserved for producers (finance directors) or auditors (technical partners from large accounting firms) or, more recently, career standard-setters. Despite the lip-service that standard-setters pay to the 'needs of users' it is not at all clear what various users do expect (or 'need') from accounts.

It may be difficult in practice to ensure that standard-setting boards include all important interests and opinions. For example, it might be hard to persuade someone to serve, even part-time, who did not think standards were a good idea. Yet many people do not. Perhaps encouraging the possibility of *disagreement* among board members would be a convincing test of 'general acceptability'. Should there be a 'devil's advocate' on an accounting standards board? The alternative might be a self-selecting clique sharing a minority view that they attempt to impose on everyone else.

---

6   F. A. Hayek, 'Competition as a Discovery Procedure', ch. 12 in *New Studies*, op. cit.

The old UK Accounting Standards Committee had few enforcement 'teeth': a qualified audit report or a possible reprimand from an offender's institute were regarded as too mild. Now the Review Panel can take court proceedings against any company whose accounts it believes fail to provide a true and fair view. So far the Review Panel has always managed to procure agreement to revise offending accounts without actually having to go to court. Thus the ultimate sanction is to trigger the government's enforcement procedure, under the Companies Act. Some of the ASB's proposals, however, are still voluntary, such as the Operating and Financial Review (OFR), though the government intends to make it compulsory for larger companies.

Government agencies

Given a flourishing UK accounting profession, why should the government take on itself the task of issuing detailed rules with respect to measurement in accounting, which is what it now does in the Companies Act? Clearly it can muster the powers of enforcement, at least on paper, though it rarely seems to use them. But do governments really have a comparative advantage in accounting, where the key requirements are honesty and competence? The European Commission's accounts, for instance, are probably unequalled in the Western world for corruption and fraud. Solomons refers to 'the dismal record of government agencies in regulating accounting in such fields as transportation and insurance'.[7]

In 1994 the British government finally decided to switch over

---

7 Solomons, *Making Accounting Policy*, op. cit., p. 28.

from cash to accrual ('resource') accounting, well over a century after commercial accounting did so. Far from leading the way in accounting, the government had been using its coercive powers to hold back organisations that wanted to make this sensible change years earlier.

The same year also saw the 25th anniversary of the state monopoly Post Office (then including telephones) first having independent professional accountants audit its annual accounts. Before then the Auditor-General, a civil servant, had done the job. The result, in 1969, had been an eloquent comment on the quality of public sector accounting: no fewer than two full pages for one of the most heavily qualified audit opinions in living memory.

In the market there is often a clear benefit from *potential* competition. So also there may be a clear cost from *potential* government interference. Governments' notorious propensity to meddle has sometimes led accounting bodies to take pre-emptive action, for example by starting to issue accounting standards for which there is little demand.

Costs of accounting regulation

In the UK the ASB develops exposure drafts for comment (sometimes after discussion papers) and then issues standards, which the Review Panel 'enforces'. The Financial Reporting Council spends less than £3 million a year, of which nearly two-thirds represents staff costs. This is 'about one-tenth of one per cent of aggregate audit fees for the company sector'.[8] Funding for the ASB

---

8   Geoff and Gay Meeks, *Towards a cost-benefit analysis of accounting regulation*, ICAEW Centre for Business Performance, 2002, pp. 4, 10.

comes from three main sources: the accountancy profession, via the Consultative Committee of Accountancy Bodies; the government, mainly the Department of Trade and Industry; and the City, mainly the London Stock Exchange.

The International Accounting Standards Board's budget, which includes travel costs, was £12 million in 2002. But even this is small. The direct costs of 'producing' accounting standards in the USA are somewhat larger, but still low. The FASB's costs in 2000 totalled $24 million (about £16 million), to which we should add part of the SEC's costs. But relative to size of population, or to the market value of listed equities, US costs seem similar to those in the UK.

Thus the *direct* costs of producing and enforcing accounting standards are currently not very large. For the three main standard-setters they amount in total to well under £50 million a year.

In addition there are indirect costs for reporting entities and auditors who have to comply with accounting standards, as well as for users of accounts. In total these costs are probably much larger, though difficult to estimate. For example, it has been estimated[9] that the 2002 Sarbanes-Oxley Act may add between $3 million and $8 million in annual compliance costs for a Fortune 500 company. If that is right, for the 500 as a whole that could mean at least $1.5 billion a year.

Lomax predicted in 1987, at the time of the inception of the Financial Services Act:

> The direct costs of the new systems will be very great ...
> about £20 million a year, and the internal costs in the City
> institutions could easily amount to five times as much ...

---

9   *Fortune*, 8 September 2003, p. 21.

The number of compliance officers operating in the City is likely to amount to well over a thousand. … Some tens of millions of pieces of paper will be floating around the City as a result of this new system. The cost is therefore very high, and indeed is *substantially greater than any identified losses* suffered by investors in public 'scandals' in recent years (emphasis added).[10]

A subsequent study of the securities industry[11] reckoned that indirect costs amounted to just over four times as much as direct costs; but found that direct costs were over £50 million a year, much higher than Lomax's estimate. Some of the indirect costs might have occurred even without regulation, so probably not all of them are incremental.

The DTI reckoned[12] in 2003 that compulsory application of IAS to all unlisted UK companies (as well as to the 2,700 listed companies) would result in *one-off* costs for them of between £576 million and £1,400 million. This seems a huge amount, and with a huge margin of error too (roughly £1,000 million $+/-$ 40 per cent).

In fact we have little idea of the indirect costs of complying with financial regulations, including accounting standards. The few existing studies suggest they may be about four times the direct costs.

It is now widely recognised that regulation may do more harm

10   David Lomax, 'London Markets after the Financial Services Act', Butterworth, 1987, quoted in Goodhart, op. cit.

11   Julian R. Franks, Stephen M. Schaefer and Michael D. Staunton, 'The direct and compliance costs of financial regulation', *Journal of Banking & Finance*, 21, 1998, pp. 1,547–72.

12   *Financial Times* report, 17 July 2003.

than good, as a recent publication by the Better Regulation Task Force emphasised:

> For example, certain regulatory bodies who pass on their costs to those they regulate may have little incentive to minimise these costs ... Some may want to impose high standards in order to avoid blame if things go wrong. And there may be little pressure to withdraw from regulatory areas, unlike in a competitive market where rivals will restrain growth. Also there are always incentives to do new things, so regulatory bodies often tend to expand. There is also the possibility of 'regulatory capture', where a regulator becomes sympathetic to the interests of those they [*sic*] regulate, and acts to protect their interests.
>
> Furthermore, it is easy to underestimate the costs of regulation, which include effects on entrepreneurial behaviour and innovation, as well as the costs of the regulatory body and the compliance costs of the people being regulated. Regulation often makes it difficult or costly for companies to take account of technical innovations, and may crowd out market solutions to problems.[13]

George Soros provides a useful reminder of the flaws of regulators:

> ... regulators are also participants. There is a natural tendency to regard them as superhuman beings who somehow stand outside and above the economic process and intervene only when the participants have made a mess of it. That is not the case. They also are human, all too human. They operate with imperfect understanding and their activities have unintended consequences. Indeed,

---

13 Better Regulation Task Force, 'Imaginative Thinking for Better Regulation', September 2003, p. 19.

they seem to adjust to changing circumstances less well than those who are motivated by profit and loss, so that regulations are generally designed to prevent the last mishap, not the next one.[14]

Cost–benefit analysis

To justify regulation its benefits must exceed its various costs. But measuring either total costs or benefits seems to be extremely difficult. Much of modern UK financial regulation stems from the 1984 Gower Report,[15] whose author rejected any sort of cost–benefit analysis on the grounds that he was not competent to undertake it and doubted whether it was practical.

One of the ASB's Fundamental Guidelines[16] is: 'To issue accounting standards only when the expected benefits exceed the perceived costs ... [but] the Board recognises that reliable cost/benefit calculations are seldom possible.' So are we to assume that at least in respect of the twenty Financial Reporting Standards issued so far they *have* been possible? Or has the ASB just gone ahead and issued standards anyway? Regulators, whether of accounts or medicines or railways or national security, usually want to avoid being blamed if things go wrong. In the absence of reliable cost–benefit estimates they may often be tempted to *over*-regulate.

There is an extensive American literature on the regulation

14 George Soros, *The Alchemy of Finance*, Weidenfeld & Nicolson, London, 1988, p. 85.
15 James Gower, *Review of Investor Protection*, Cmnd. 9125, HMSO, 1984, para. 1.16.
16 ASB, *Statement of Principles for Financial Reporting*, Exposure Draft 1995, Appendix 1, p. 129.

of accounting which helps to highlight the issues, although the outcome is remarkably inconclusive.

- According to Watts and Zimmerman: 'The SEC spends virtually none of its budget in systematically assessing the costs and benefits of regulation.'[17]
- Foster says: ' … it is far from obvious that a policy body such as the SEC or the FASB can regulate information production so as to achieve an efficient allocation of resources … '[18]
- And Beaver concludes: 'In the absence of evidence, the desirability of having a regulated environment is an open issue.'[19]

So it seems the whole paraphernalia of accounting standards is based on faith, not on evidence.[20] There has been little serious work on cost–benefit analysis and, despite occasional lip-service, most regulators seem to pay hardly any attention to it.

An accounting regulator from hell

The road to hell is paved with good intentions. So we may speculate how an accounting regulator from hell might behave. If actual present-day accounting standard-setters are anything to go by, she would yield to ten (not seven) deadly sins:

17 Ross L. Watts and Jerold L. Zimmerman, *Positive Accounting Theory*, Prentice-Hall, Englewood Cliffs, NJ, 1986, ch. 7.

18 George Foster, *Financial Statement Analysis*, Prentice-Hall, Englewood Cliffs, NJ, 2nd edn, 1986, ch.2.

19 William H. Beaver, *Financial Reporting: An Accounting Revolution*, Prentice-Hall, Englewood Cliffs, NJ, 3rd edn, 1998, p. 168.

20 Thomas S. Kuhn, *The Structure of Scientific Revolutions*, University of Chicago Press, 2nd edn, p. 158.

1. She would assume or assert without evidence that there was a 'need' for regulation.

2. She would implicitly compare actual market results with 'perfect' outcomes (the 'nirvana' fallacy) and attribute any 'shortfall' to absence of (sufficient) regulation.

3. Having promised only to introduce standards if the benefits exceeded the costs, in practice she would scorn to compare the two. If she did attempt to do so, she would consider only direct costs and ignore compliance and indirect and longer-term costs.

4. Hence she would shift from voluntary guidelines ('suggestions') to compulsory directions ('instructions') without even noticing the difference, let alone thinking it mattered.

5. She would then impose rules that did not have general acceptance either from preparers or users of accounts. The more complex the task, and the more individual the judgement involved, the more complex the regulation would be.

6. She would fail to revise or repeal damaging or out-of-date rules long after their inadequacies had become apparent. 'Better to have bad regulations than no regulations.'

7. She would seek to shut off possible escape by arranging a worldwide monopoly of regulators under some label such as 'international harmonisation'.

8. She would claim, on the basis of very little evidence, that this would reduce companies' cost of capital. (If this were true, it would provide sufficient commercial incentive for companies to choose themselves to converge on existing 'best practice'.)

9. In order to avoid blame if anything should 'go wrong', she would tend to over-regulate.

10. Finally, of course, if despite all her 'expert' and well-meant efforts anything *did* go wrong, her proposed solution would be … still more regulation.

9   CONCLUSIONS

Drawing on the earlier analysis, this chapter discusses whether accounting standards should:

- be compulsory or voluntary;
- deal with measurement as well as disclosure;
- apply to small and non-business entities as well as to listed and traded companies.

My minimalist preference is for very short voluntary guidelines ('Suggestions') on basic matters of disclosure for publicly listed companies only. I propose that we have no compulsory accounting standards ('Instructions'), no standards on measurement and no standards at all for unlisted or small companies or for non-business entities.

Instructions

Members of the Accounting Standards Board and other standard-setters are trying to overturn orthodox accounting. They are revolutionaries.[1] Table 5 lists four contrasts:

---

1   D. R. Myddelton, 'Orthodox versus Revolutionary Accounting', *Journal of Applied Accounting Research*, 3(II), October 1996, pp. 17–36.

Table 5 **Orthodox versus revolutionary accounting**

	Orthodox		*Revolutionary*
Purpose	Stewardship	v.	Decision-usefulness
Audience	Existing shareholders	v.	Existing and potential investors
Source of legitimacy	General acceptance	v.	Compulsory standards
Basis of measurement	Historical cost	v.	Current value

In each case the ASB shuns the orthodox option, though it soothingly talks about a 'continuation of evolutionary change'. Revolutionaries need coercion, which is why the ASB insists on compulsory accounting standards ('Instructions') rather than the voluntary 'Suggestions' that Dearing proposed (a fact of which at least one senior ASB official[2] was not even aware). Making standards compulsory rather than voluntary no doubt increases the power of the standard-setters, which may appeal to them.

Chapter 4 discussed arguments in favour of accounting standards. Most of them seem weak, especially in the longer term. It would be ironic if attempts to prevent short-termist company accounting turned out themselves to lead to serious long-term damage. It is of course possible that accounting standards do on balance raise the 'quality' of company accounts, even if perhaps by less than is sometimes claimed. But not all improvements in accounting are caused by standards, nor do all standards necessarily cause improvements. There seems to be little evidence of damage to investors in the absence of accounting standards, or of any reduction in damage as a result of their appearance. The fact is we cannot tell to what extent accounting standards may have

---

2   Andrew Lennard, at ACCA 1999 conference to discuss the Statement of Principles.

helped to prevent trouble. What is clear is that, with or without standards, accounts will sometimes be faulty.

Even if 'compulsory' standards were to continue, it might be worth retaining the IASC's approach (also followed by EU directives) of allowing alternative treatments. This alone does much to dispel the misleading notion that there can be a single 'correct answer'.

There is wide circulation of exposure drafts before issuing accounting standards. But response levels to exposure drafts seem fairly low, perhaps because nobody expects the standard-setters to take much notice of anything but massive industry lobbying. Certainly the ASB ignored most of the widespread criticism of its draft Statement of Principles, even from the main UK accounting firms.

Having only a single source of accounting standards makes it vulnerable to 'capture'. Governments may be tempted to interfere if they dislike a proposed Instruction, as has happened in both the UK and the USA. Compulsory standards provide a channel for such interference which would not otherwise exist.

Standard-setters need to consult widely if they are to gain acceptance. That may be important when it comes to enforcement. Another traffic analogy may be relevant. If most motorists, rightly or wrongly, regard some speed limits on roads as being too low, many drivers may be inclined to ignore them, and enforcement in the absence of general acceptance may generate a hostile reaction.

An Instruction-issuing board has to market standards as well as produce them. Indeed, Instruction-setting can be highly political, possibly[3] even involving deliberate ambiguities in the

---

3   See, for instance, Gore, op. cit., p. 103.

language of accounting standards or supporting documents so as to be acceptable to people holding diametrically opposed views. A recent UK example might be the failure in the ASB's discussion document on goodwill to specify under precisely what 'special and limited circumstances' companies could use the novel 'capitalisation and annual review method'. The subsequent working paper[4] continued to fudge the issue.

The way an Instruction-issuing board works can make a difference. For example, who appoints members of the board? Who sets the agenda? What majority is needed to issue an Instruction? What happens if new members disagree with the view of former members? Must they retain an Instruction which could not now gain sufficient votes from board members? Where only one accounting method is allowed there will be an abrupt transition when the party line changes. One day the board requires Method A, the next day it forbids Method A and substitutes Method B. That seems unsatisfactory.

There is also the question of whether the board, consisting of up to a dozen full-time paid members, could choose to do nothing in return for their pay. Or must they go on issuing and revising accounting standards even if, for the time being, they think their work is more or less complete? If so, might that lead to over-regulation? Is a standard-setting board a 'venture' for accounting purposes or a 'going concern' with an infinite life?

Some people think the ASB's Financial Reporting Standards since 1990 have been far too detailed, more than 1,500 pages for twenty standards (excluding FRSSE). The ASB claims the length

---

4   ASB, *Goodwill & Intangible Assets*, working paper for discussion at public hearing, June 1995.

of the standards is in response to consumer demand. (A rough percentage split is: Essential 20; Explanation 24; Examples 23; User Assistance 33.) But much of that 'demand' arises because the standards are compulsory. If they were voluntary, failure to follow them to the letter would not necessarily mean failure to give 'a true and fair view': that may also be the case with compulsory standards, but we don't know, and in today's climate many auditors would rather be safe than sorry.

Compulsory accounting standards are not worthwhile, I believe, because the advantages of compulsion are few and the disadvantages many. That would remain so even if all the direct and compliance 'costs' were zero.

Suggestions

A recent revision of the Operating and Financial Review said it was designed to formulate and develop best practice, intended to have persuasive rather than mandatory force. What an enlightened approach. Would that all accounting standards were as modest! If some standards are not persuasive, why insist on everyone obeying them? Sir David Tweedie himself believes that some US standards are 'pretty bad'.[5]

Voluntary accounting standards ('Suggestions') avoid all four drawbacks of compulsory standards ('Instructions'). They leave the preparers and auditors of accounts free to exercise professional judgement; they permit competition in ideas and would not inhibit further evolution; nor would they rule out any accounting

---

5   Donna L. Street, 'An Interview with Sir David Tweedie', *Journal of International Financial Management and Accounting*, 13(1), 2002, p. 85.

methods providing a true and fair view. Freedom to choose would not 'legitimise' bad accounting. And being less 'official', it would be less likely that Suggestions would unduly raise public expectations.

Those in favour of Instructions might argue that voluntary Suggestions cannot overcome the first three problems discussed in Chapter 4: dishonesty of preparers, lack of independence of auditors, and possible damage to investors. Instructions don't really overcome the first two either, and I dispute the existence of the third on a significant scale. On the other hand, Suggestions can probably fulfil two of the six aims of Instructions. They may be as able as Instructions to provide guidance on complex accounting issues and (without requiring it) help to develop uniform language and layout in accounts. Finally, comparing the accounts of different companies, however 'desirable', will always be problematic whether we have accounting standards or not.

In the absence of standards, how could one tell whether a specific accounting practice was 'generally acceptable' as giving a 'true and fair' view? Regular surveys might help to provide such evidence. They can be expensive, but surely a lot cheaper than standards. In specific disputed cases, possibly some form of 'jury', perhaps only half a dozen strong, could be drawn from lay people working in some area of accounting or business, taking evidence from leading accountants of the day. Such a group need not be 'politically correct'; indeed, Devlin[6] says it is the so-called perversity of juries which justifies their existence. For a start, we might ask a jury to review the 'conceptual framework' on which standard-setters seem so keen. I doubt if it would survive such a test.

---

6   Patrick Devlin, *The Judge*, Oxford University Press, 1979, p. 131.

Suggestions need not aim to cover every possible case in detail, so they can be fairly short and simple. As examples, Appendices 4 and 5 set out two possible 'Suggestions' on Goodwill and Inflation Accounting. These are both difficult measurement problems in accounting, yet the two Suggestions comprise only a page or two each, whereas FRSs on these two topics, on present form, might well exceed a hundred pages each. That is a huge difference. If desired, similar brief Suggestions could cover other important accounting measurement topics.

The idea of competing Suggestions has some appeal. The absence of a single source would reduce the temptation for an Instruction-issuing board to claim undue 'authority'. Indeed, it might be a good idea to issue Suggestions under the name of individual authors – mortals, so to speak – rather than some official board. That would emphasise the fallibility of any such documents, whereas the current regime seems more inclined to hint at the opposite without quite being so foolish as to explicitly claim infallibility. Dye and Sunder[7] discuss the idea of 'competition' between FASB and IASB standards; but they assume that either would need to be subject to SEC approval, which rather misses the point of real competition.

People would no doubt accuse Suggestions of 'lacking teeth', which of course they would – on purpose. They would be available to help preparers and auditors of accounts, but being entirely voluntary there would be no need for any enforcement mechanism. Hence they could be provided by one or more of the professional accounting bodies, perhaps even by an International Accounting Suggestions Board.

7   Ronald A. Dye and Shyam Sunder, 'Why Not Allow FASB and IASB Standards to Compete in the US?', *Accounting Horizons*, 15(3), September 2001, pp. 257–71.

There would still be pressure for listed companies to follow 'best practice'; and those that notably failed to do so would risk losing credit and reputation as a result. True, this approach excludes the Review Panel swooping to force offenders to 'correct' their accounts. But it leaves the way open for an independent profession to help accounting to evolve freely.

It might not be long before some 'representative' body was tempted to 'coordinate' the various Suggestions, with the feeble excuse that 'otherwise the government might step in' – even though when government has directly interfered in accounting the result has usually been disastrous. It goes without saying that such coordination should be vigorously resisted.

Even if Suggestions were voluntary, there would probably still be an exposure draft stage. So they could cost as much to produce as Instructions. Indeed, the total cost might even be more, if there were several 'competing' sources of Suggestions. On the other hand, compliance costs might be a good deal less. In my view voluntary Suggestions would have most of the advantages and none of the disadvantages of compulsory Instructions.

Standards on disclosure, not on measurement

The arguments for standards on disclosure are not quite the same as for standards on measurement. We would be better off without any standards on accounting measurement. The cure is worse than the disease. Company law already requires accounts to give 'a true and fair view'. In stark contrast to the present system, with its two thousand pages of very detailed regulations, one might simply leave it at that. Where audits are required, the message might be: 'Anything goes – if your auditors agree and you say what you've done.' If markets value extra disclosure, companies themselves have an incentive to provide it and coercion is superfluous.

Thus voluntary guidelines could emphasise the need for adequate disclosure but not try to prescribe the methods of measurement. This is hardly a new idea. As long ago as 1932 an AICPA Committee commented as follows to the New York Stock Exchange on two choices:

> The first is the selection by competent authority out of the body of acceptable methods in vogue today of detailed sets of rules which would become binding on all corporations of a given class … The arguments against … are, however, overwhelming.
>
> The more practicable alternative would be to leave every corporation free to choose its own methods of accounting within … very broad limits … but require disclosure of the methods employed and consistency in their application from year to year … Within quite wide limits it is relatively unimportant to the investor what precise rules or conventions a corporation [adopts] in reporting its earnings if he knows what method is being followed … consistently from year to year. [8]

This approach has several advantages. It allows accountants to exercise their professional skill and judgement in preparing company accounts that will give a true and fair view consistently over time. It does not imply (falsely) that comparisons between the accounts of different companies are possible. And it does not encourage standard-setters to get bogged down in absurdly lengthy and detailed attempts to prescribe 'correct' methods of measurement. There is evidence[9] to suggest that institutional investors are

---

8 Quoted in May, *Financial Accounting*, op. cit., appendix to ch. iv, p. 76.
9 Richard Barker, *Institutional Investors, Accounting Information and the ASB*, ICAS, 2001, p. 29.

more concerned about levels of disclosure than about underlying differences in recognition and measurement.

The effect of such a sensible proposal could perhaps be to retain some of the legislation in the Companies Act dealing with disclosure, for example requiring accounts:

- to show corresponding amounts for the previous year;
- to split equity between paid-up share capital, retained profits and other reserves;
- to disclose separately cumulative depreciation provided on fixed assets;
- to disclose separately tax on profits and interest on borrowings.

But scrapping standards on measurement would mean dropping Sections 16 to 34 of Schedule 4 of the Companies Act 1985 dealing with accounting rules, many of which were included as a result of the EU's Fourth Directive. I would also be quite happy to scrap Sections 6 to 8 of Schedule 4, the twelve pages dealing with alternative permitted formats of accounts, which also stemmed from the Fourth Directive.

In addition I would also withdraw at least twenty of the thirty extant UK accounting standards (including SSAP 24 and FRSSE), containing a total of more than 1,200 pages. That would leave perhaps ten UK standards dealing with disclosure, as shown in Table 6 below.

The three SSAPs listed contain 25 pages in total. But the seven remaining FRSs should be reduced to a fraction of their present combined length of more than five hundred pages. Voluntary suggestions simply outlining the key points from all ten of the

Table 6 **UK disclosure standards that could remain**

	pages	
SSAP 5	2	Value Added Tax
SSAP 17	7	Post-balance-sheet events
SSAP 25	16	Segmental reporting
FRS 1	71	Cash flow statements
FRS 3	57	Reporting financial performance
FRS 4	75	Capital instruments
FRS 8	37	Related party disclosures
FRS 13	165	Derivatives (disclosures)
FRS 14	61	Earnings per share
FRS 18	74	Accounting policies

The international equivalents are: IAS 1, 7, 8, 10, 14, 24, 32 and 33. (Two UK standards have no direct international equivalents.)

above standards should require only a few pages in total. (See my attempt in Appendix 6, which comprises in all only seven pages.) If this is thought to be going too far, then perhaps elements of disclosure in other standards could be restored.

Small enterprises

Few people suggest having significantly different measurement rules for the accounts of small companies, though there may be an argument for less disclosure for small companies. For smaller companies, shorter and simpler standards might often suffice – or even none at all. Not long ago an ICAEW working party[10] proposed exempting small companies from all but five accounting standards.

Even if there were still some voluntary disclosure and/or presentation guidelines for listed companies, in my view unlisted

---

10 CCAB Consultative Document, *Exemptions from Standards on Grounds of Size or Public Interest*, November 1994.

companies and smaller enterprises should be exempted from all of them. They, like non-business entities, are not really organisations for which accounting standards, in anything like their present form, are suitable. Their accounts could still be required to give a true and fair view. But there is no need to have thousands of pages of accounting standards to achieve that.

On balance …

In the nine years since *Accountants without Standards?*, the precursor to this Hobart Paper, was published, the volume of UK accounting standards (including company law) has risen from about 800 pages to about 2,000 pages. Who would have predicted that outcome in 1995? If things continue at the same rate, where will we be in another thirty years' time? (Answer: over 40,000 pages!)

There is much in Arthur Seldon's view that we should accept more risks of under-regulation. And I agree with Baxter:

> A terse list of minimum requirements, such as [was] given in the British [1948] Companies Act, works well and leaves honest men tolerably free to think and experiment. It provides a floor not a ceiling. Freedom is necessary for progress. 'Freedom' here means the absence, not merely of crude tyranny, but also of benevolent authority that makes us respectful to some ideas and hostile to others.[11]

Nor would a 'retreat from standards' give the wrong signal. On the contrary, the kind of 'authority' claimed for accounting standards, especially those dealing with measurements, is unwise

11 Baxter, 2nd edn, op. cit., p. 416.

in intellectual and commercial matters. Members of the public (including journalists) should recognise the limits of company accounts. In particular, it is far easier to compare results within a single company over a period of years than between different companies. That may be unfortunate, but it is a fact.

Governments should steel themselves not to interfere in matters they do not understand and which they are ill equipped to manage. Where professional bodies want to offer help to their members in coping with complex matters they should provide technical notes on a strictly 'take it or leave it' basis. Even official 'Recommendations' strive for, and tend to get, more authority than is suitable in what should be both an independent profession and a body of independent professionals.

Compulsory Instructions concerning measurement may seem tempting in the short term, since they make it look as if someone is 'doing something'. But laissez-faire too has advantages. Instructions have insidious effects in the longer term, which may not become fully apparent until it is almost too late to reverse the trend. Standards telling companies which accounting methods they must use can legitimise bad accounting and prohibit good accounting.

The present chairman of the International Accounting Standards Board has written: 'In an ideal world, accounting standards would not be necessary.'[12] I couldn't agree more.

---

12   David Tweedie and Geoffrey Whittington, *The Debate on Inflation Accounting*, Cambridge University Press, 1984, p. 327.

APPENDIX 1

UK ACCOUNTING STANDARDS AS AT 31 DECEMBER 2003

Statements of Standard Accounting Practice (Accounting Standards Committee)

SSAP	Topic	First issued	Pages
4	Government grants	April 1974	9
5	Value Added Tax	April 1974	2
9	Stocks and long-term contracts	May 1975	23
13	Research and development	December 1977	11
17	Post-balance-sheet events	August 1980	7
19	Investment properties	November 1981	10
20	Foreign currency translation	April 1983	14
21	Leases & hire purchase contracts	August 1984	11
24	Pension costs*	May 1988	
<u>25</u>	Segmental reporting	June 1990	<u>16</u>
10			103

* SSAP 24 will be superseded by FRS 17, the introduction of which has been delayed.

Financial Reporting Standards
(Accounting Standards Board)

FRS	Topic	First issued	Pages
1	Cash flow statements	September 1991	71
2	Subsidiary undertakings	July 1992	75
3	Reporting financial performance	October 1992	57
4	Capital instruments	December 1993	75
5	Reporting the substance of transactions	April 1994	160
6	Acquisitions and mergers	September 1994	60
7	Fair values on acquisition	September 1994	57
8	Related party transactions	December 1995	37
9	Associates and joint ventures	November 1997	81
10	Goodwill and intangible assets	December 1997	77
11	Impairment of fixed assets	July 1998	63
12	Provisions and contingencies	September 1998	88
13	Derivatives: disclosures	September 1998	165
14	Earnings per share	September 1998	61
15	Tangible fixed assets	February 1999	96
16	Current tax	October 1999	27
17	Retirement benefits	October 2000	81
18	Accounting policies	December 2000	74
19	Deferred tax	December 2000	112
**	Smaller entities (FRSSE)	Regular revisions	<u>204</u>
			1,721

** This FRS is unnumbered.

APPENDIX 2

INTERNATIONAL ACCOUNTING
STANDARDS AS AT 31 DECEMBER 2003

	Topic	First issued	Pages
IAS	Framework	1989	38
IAS 1	Presentation of accounts	1975/97	44
2	Inventories	1976/93	12
7	Cash flow statements	1979/92	27
8	Changes in accounting policies, etc.	1979/93	25
10	Post-balance-sheet events	1980/94*	10
11	Construction contracts	1980/93	20
12	Taxes on income	1981/96	68
14	Segment reporting	1983/97	41
16	Property, plant and equipment	1983/93–98	27
17	Leases	1984/97	25
18	Revenue	1984/93	25
19	Employee benefits	1985/95–98	80
20	Government grants	1984/94*	11
21	Changes in foreign exchange rates	1985/93	17
22	Business combinations	1985/95–98	50
23	Borrowing costs	1986/93	10
24	Related party transactions	1986/94*	9
26	Reporting by retirement benefit plans	1988/94*	14
27	Consolidated accounts	1990/94*	12
28	Investments in associates	1990/98	13
29	Hyper-inflationary economies	1990/94*	11
30	Disclosures in banks' accounts	1991/94*	17
31	Interests in joint ventures	1992/98	17
32	Financial instruments: disclosure	1996/98	54
33	Earnings per share	1997	24
34	Interim financial reporting	1998	34
35	Discontinuing operations	1998	30

	Topic	First issued	Pages
36	Impairment of assets	1998	77
37	Provisions and contingencies	1998	46
38	Intangible assets	1998	48
39	Financial instruments: measurement	1999	80
40	Investment property	2000	27
41	Agriculture	2001	<u>25</u>
			1,030

(total excludes IAS Framework, as not officially a standard)

IFRS 1	First-time adoption of IASs	June 2003

Where two dates are given (e.g. 1986/94) this denotes date of first issue followed by date of revision, except where the second date is followed by an asterisk, which indicates reformatting without material revision at this time. Where three dates are given (e.g. 1985/95–98) the third date relates to further revision. Fourteen IASs were 'improved' in 2003: 1, 2, 8, 10, 16, 17, 21, 24, 27, 28, 31, 32, 33, 40.

APPENDIX 3

CONFLICTS BETWEEN THE COMPANIES ACT 1985 AND UK ACCOUNTING STANDARDS

The following conflicts between the Companies Act 1985 and UK Accounting Standards are listed in order of the paragraph numbers in Schedule 4 of the Companies Act 1985.

1. Para. 3 (2):

'… the following shall not be treated as assets in any company's balance sheet … (c) costs of research'.

This contradicts SSAP 13 on Research and Development, para. 16:

'Fixed assets may be acquired or constructed in order to provide facilities for research and/or development activities. The use of such fixed assets usually extends over a number of accounting periods and accordingly they should be capitalised and written off over their useful life.'

2. Para. 3 (7):

'Every profit and loss account of a company shall show separately … (b) the aggregate amount of any dividends paid and proposed.'

With respect to dividends proposed but not yet declared, this does not accord with FRS 5, para. 4:

'Liabilities are defined as follows: Liabilities are an entity's obligations to transfer economic benefits as a result of past transactions or events.'

3. Para. 12:

'The amount of any item shall be determined on a prudent basis, and in particular (a) only profits realised at the balance sheet date shall be included in the profit and loss account ... '

Profits in respect of work-in-progress on long-term contracts are probably not 'realised' at the balance sheet date, yet SSAP 9 on Stocks and Long-term Contracts, para. 29, requires such profit to be included where it can be assessed 'with reasonable certainty'. (IAS 11, para. 22, is similar.) The Companies Act prohibits the inclusion of profits on long-term contracts in the current asset amount shown for stocks and work-in-progress:

Para. 22: '... the amount to be included in respect of any current asset shall be its purchase price or production cost'.

Para. 23: '(or net realisable value if lower)'.

Hence awkward arrangements have been made in amending SSAP 9, to show as debtors any profit on work-in-progress on long-term contracts.

4. Para. 12:

'The amount of any item shall be determined on a prudent basis, and in particular ... (b) all liabilities and losses which have arisen or are likely to arise in respect of the financial

> year to which the accounts relate or a previous financial year
> shall be taken into account …'

But SSAP 24 on Pension Costs, para. 80, requires so-called past service costs to be spread out 'over the remaining service lives of current employees in the scheme'. This hardly seems to be 'a prudent basis'. (FRS 17 has not yet completely superseded SSAP 24.)

Indeed, para. 82 of SSAP 24 explicitly restricts the application of a prudent basis of accounting, apparently in contradiction to the Companies Act:

> 'In strictly limited circumstances prudence may require that
> a material deficit be recognised over a period shorter than
> the expected remaining service lives of current employees in
> the scheme. Such circumstances are limited to those where
> a major event or transaction has occurred which has not
> been allowed for in the actuarial assumptions, is outside the
> normal scope of those assumptions and has necessitated
> the payment of significant additional contributions to the
> pension scheme.'

5. *Para. 18*:

> 'In case of any fixed asset which has a limited useful
> economic life, the amount of (a) its purchase price or
> production cost; or (b) where it is estimated that any such
> asset will have a residual value at the end of the period of
> its useful economic life, its purchase price or production
> cost less that estimated residual value; shall be reduced
> by provisions for depreciation calculated to write off that
> amount systematically over the period of the asset's useful
> economic life.'

This is inconsistent with FRS 15 on Depreciation, p. 13, which defines residual value as: 'the realisable value of the asset at the end of its useful economic life, based on prices prevailing at the date of acquisition or revaluation, where this has taken place'.

The Companies Act requires the *expected money amount* of the realisable value to be deducted from the purchase price or production cost in determining the amount of depreciation. It does not say anything about 'prices prevailing at the date of acquisition'; nor, in a system using money as the accounting unit of measurement, would this seem justifiable. (IAS 16's definition of residual value *is* consistent with the UK Companies Act.) The use of Constant Purchasing Power accounting would overcome this problem.

6. Para. 18 (as quoted in (5) above):
This is inconsistent with SSAP 19 on Investment Properties which, in para. 10, forbids the depreciation of investment properties, except for leaseholds with less than twenty years to run.

7. Para. 20 (1):

> '…an amount may only be included in a company's
> balance sheet in respect of development costs in special
> circumstances.'

SSAP 13 on Research and Development permits the capitalisation of development costs which meet certain 'stringent criteria' set out in paras 10 to 12. It seems unlikely that meeting these criteria in SSAP 13 would be considered *automatically* to amount to the 'special circumstances' called for by the Companies Act. (IAS 38 *requires* the capitalisation of development costs in certain circumstances.)

8. Para. 21 (2):

> '… the amount of the consideration for any goodwill
> acquired by a company shall be reduced by provisions
> for depreciation calculated to write off that amount
> systematically over a period chosen by the directors of the
> company'.

Para. 21 (3)

> 'The period chosen shall not exceed the useful economic life
> of the goodwill in question.'

FRS 10, para. 17, says: 'Where goodwill and intangible assets are regarded as having indefinite useful economic lives, they should not be amortised.' (IAS 38 does not currently contain a similar exemption: it requires amortisation of goodwill, in line with the UK Companies Act.)

APPENDIX 4

SUGGESTION – ACCOUNTING FOR GOODWILL

- Include purchased goodwill (including related intangible assets) at cost in the balance sheet until fully written off, but not non-purchased ('internal') goodwill.
- Amortise the cost of purchased goodwill through the profit and loss account, using the straight-line method or any more suitable accelerated method.
- Amortise the cost of purchased goodwill to nil over its life, with a maximum of twenty years. Review each year to determine whether to reduce (never to extend) the life.
- Review each year to assess whether the current value of purchased goodwill has fallen below the book amount. If so, write down at once through the profit and loss account. Do not revalue purchased goodwill upwards.
- Write off any relevant unamortised goodwill through the profit and loss account against the disposal proceeds of any business segment.
- Show the amount of goodwill resulting from each acquisition during the year.
- Disclose details of purchased goodwill as for tangible fixed assets.
- On the adoption of this Suggestion, reinstate in the balance sheet any purchased goodwill earlier deducted from reserves. Calculate the amounts as if this Suggestion had always been followed and explain what they refer to.

APPENDIX 5

SUGGESTION: ACCOUNTING FOR INFLATION

- Show results for the period and the financial position at the end of the period in terms of Constant Purchasing Power (CPP) units of a stated date.
- Use the Retail Prices Index to translate unadjusted accounts.
- Disclose separately the purchasing power loss or gain on monetary items.
- If necessary redate corresponding amounts for previous periods into the same units of account as the current period.
- Outline the method used to restate accounts originally prepared in foreign currencies.
- Translate non-monetary items by restating them in proportion to the change in the purchasing power of money between the date of their acquisition or revaluation and the date of the CPP units. Translate monetary items only if the date of the CPP units differs from the balance sheet date.
- After translation of non-monetary items, apply to current assets the test of 'lower of (translated) cost and (translated) net realisable value'. Similarly further provision may be needed after translation of fixed assets.

Definitions

Translation restates money amounts into terms of CPP units.

Unadjusted accounts are those prepared under established conventions using money as the unit of account, including those in which some assets have been revalued.

Monetary items are assets, liabilities or capital, the amounts of which are fixed in terms of money regardless of changes in purchasing power.

Redating restates CPP units of one date into terms of CPP units of another date.

Non-monetary items are all items other than monetary items, except equity share capital and reserves.

Revaluation substitutes current values of non-monetary items for historical costs.

APPENDIX 6

POSSIBLE SUGGESTIONS ON 'DISCLOSURE'

Accounting policies (FRS 18)

- Adopt accounting policies that enable accounts to give a true and fair view. Prepare accounts on a going-concern basis unless management intends to cease trading. Prepare accounts on an accrual basis (except for the cash flow statement).
- Disclose each material accounting policy and material details of any change.
- Accounting policies should be: relevant for assessing management's stewardship, consistent over time, free from deliberate bias, prudent. Inappropriate accounting policies are not rectified either by disclosure of policies used or by notes.

Capital instruments (FRS 4)

- Classify all capital instruments in the balance sheet as liabilities, shareholders' funds or minority interests. Disclose convertible debt separately under liabilities. Disclose separately borrowings falling due for repayment on demand or in less than one year. Analyse shareholders' funds between equity interests and non-equity interests.

- *Non-equity shares* are shares:
  - (a) any of whose rights to receive payments are for a limited amount;
  - (b) any of whose rights to share in a surplus on winding-up are for a limited amount;
  - (c) which are redeemable, either according to their terms or because the holder can require their redemption.
- Summarise the rights of each class of shares, other than ordinary equity shares, as to:
  - dividends and voting;
  - dates at which shares are redeemable and amounts payable on redemption;
  - their priority and amounts receivable on a winding-up.

Cash flow statements (FRS 1)

- *Cash* means 'cash and deposits less overdrafts'.
- *Liquid resources* includes current asset investments held as readily disposable.
- *Net debt* means 'borrowings less cash and liquid resources'.
- Report cash flows for the period classified between operating, investing and financing, showing separately tax, dividends, capital expenditure, acquisitions and disposals.
- Reconcile 'operating profit' and 'net cash flow from operations' and disclose separately the movements in stocks, debtors and creditors related to operations.
- Reconcile cash movements with the movements in net debt.

Derivatives (disclosures) (FRS 13)

- Scope: all entities other than insurance companies and banks; all financial assets and liabilities, except:
  - (a) interests in subsidiary, associated and joint venture undertakings;
  - (b) employers' obligations to employees under share option and share schemes;
  - (c) pension and other post-retirement benefit assets and liabilities;
  - (d) rights and obligations arising under operating leases;
  - (e) equity shares, and warrants or options on such shares, issued by the reporting entity.
- A *financial instrument* is any contract that gives rise both to a financial asset of one entity and a financial liability or equity instrument of another entity, including both primary financial instruments and derivative financial instruments.
- A *derivative financial instrument* is a financial instrument that derives its value from the price or rate of some underlying item, such as equities, bonds, commodities, interest rates, exchange rates and stock market and other indices.
- Explain how financial instruments create or change the entity's risks.
- Disclose aggregate numerical information about: interest rate risk, currency risk, liquidity risk, and financial instruments used for trading and for hedging.

Earnings per share (FRS 14)

- Calculate *basic* earnings per share (EPS) by dividing the net profit attributable to ordinary shareholders by the weighted average number of ordinary shares outstanding during the period. Adjust the number of shares outstanding for current and previous periods to allow for bonus issues, bonus elements in a rights issue, or share splits.

- In calculating *diluted* EPS, adjust profit and number of shares for the effects of all dilutive potential ordinary shares, which should be deemed to have been converted into ordinary shares at the beginning of the period or, if later, the date of issue.
- Disclose both basic EPS and diluted EPS and reconcile the profit and number of shares.
- Reconcile any alternative method of calculating EPS with basic EPS.

Post-balance-sheet events (SSAP 17)

- Prepare accounts on the basis of conditions existing at the balance sheet date and disclose the date on which the board of directors approved the accounts.
- Post-balance-sheet events providing additional evidence of conditions existing at the balance sheet date are *adjusting events* which require changes in the amounts to be included in accounts; those concerning conditions which did not exist at that date are *non-adjusting events* which should be disclosed if non-disclosure would affect the ability of users of accounts to understand the financial position properly; and the notes should state the nature of the event and an estimate of its financial effect.

Related parties (FRS 8)

- Two or more parties are *related* when at any time during the period one party has direct or indirect control of the other or the parties are subject to common control. When another party controls the reporting entity, disclose the relationship and the name.
- The following are related parties of the reporting entity:
    - its associates and joint ventures;
    - its directors and its parent's directors;
    - its key management and those of its parent;
    - a person able to control 20 per cent or more of its voting rights;
    - members of the close family of any individual mentioned above.
- Disclose material transactions with a related party in the period, including:
    - (a) the names of the related parties and a description of their relationship;
    - (b) a description of the transactions and the amounts involved;
    - (c) any other elements necessary to understand the accounts;
    - (d) amounts due to or from related parties at the balance sheet date;
    - (e) amounts written off in respect of debts due to and from related parties.

Reporting financial performance (FRS 3)

- *Exceptional items* derive from 'ordinary' events or transactions which, by virtue of their size or incidence, the accounts need to disclose in order to give a true and fair view.

- *Extraordinary items* possess a high degree of abnormality and arise from events or transactions that are not expected to recur.
- *Earnings per share* is the profit after tax in pence per ordinary share in issue.
- Disclose each of the above separately, and also:
  - analyse turnover and operating profit between continuing operations, acquisitions and discontinued operations;
  - disclose profits or losses on sale or termination of an operation or of fixed assets;
  - reconcile in a note the opening and closing total of shareholders' funds.

Segment reporting (SSAP 25)

- A *class of business* is a distinct part of an entity that provides a separate product or service or a separate group of related products or services.
- A *geographical segment* is an area comprising an individual country or group of countries in which an entity operates, or to which it supplies products or services.
- An entity with two or more classes of business or operating in two or more geographical segments, which differ substantially from each other, should report with respect to each: turnover, operating profit, net assets and capital expenditure. Segments should be redefined when appropriate, restating previous figures.

Value Added Tax (SSAP 5)

- Turnover should exclude Value Added Tax (VAT). Include irrecoverable VAT in the cost of items disclosed separately in published accounts.

QUESTIONS FOR DISCUSSION

1. Is there a 'gap' between what the public expects and what company accounts can deliver? If so, is this because achievement is too low or because the public expects too much?

2. What are accounting standards trying to 'standardise'? Is this (a) desirable, (b) possible?

3. To what extent do you think accounting standards have achieved their aims?

4. Is there a case for advisory voluntary standards ('Suggestions') rather than compulsory standards ('Instructions') as at present? What are the pros and cons?

5. Is there a distinction between disclosure standards and measurement standards?

6. Should accounting standards apply only to listed companies or to much smaller entities too? Should accounting standards apply only to profit-seeking businesses or to non-business entities too?

7. Who should be responsible for setting accounting standards? Why?

8. To what extent should Companies Act legislation set accounting standards, rather than the Accounting Standards Board?

9. Is it desirable for accounting standards in different countries

to be 'harmonised'? Why or why not? If so, which body should be responsible?

10. Is it inevitable that the scope and extent of accounting standards should expand over the years? Why? Where will the process end?

FURTHER READING

Beaver, William H. (1998), *Financial Reporting: An Accounting Revolution*, Englewood Cliffs, NJ: Prentice-Hall, 3rd edn, especially ch. 7.

Bloom, Robert and Pieter T. Elgers (eds) (1995), *Issues in Accounting Policy*, New York: Harcourt Brace Jovanovich, 3rd edn, especially Part I (pp. 1–129).

Flower, Jon with Gabi Ebbers (2002), *Global Financial Reporting*, Palgrave.

Gore, Pelham (1992), *The FASB Conceptual Framework Project 1973–1985*, Manchester University Press.

Higson, Andrew (2003), *Corporate Financial Reporting: Theory & Practice*, London: SAGE Publications.

Jenkins (1993), *Improving business reporting – a customer focus: meeting the information needs of investors and creditors*, Comprehensive Report of the (Jenkins) Special Committee on Financial Reporting, AICPA.

Nobes, Christopher and Robert Parker (2002), *Comparative International Accounting*, Financial Times/Prentice Hall, 7th edn.

Solomons, David (1986), *Making Accounting Policy: The Quest for Credibility in Financial Reporting*, Oxford.

Wilson, Allister, Mike Davies, Matthew Curtis and Greg
  Wilkinson-Riddle (2001), *UK & International GAAP*, London:
  Butterworths Tolley for Ernst & Young, 7th edn, especially
  chs 1 and 2 (pp. 1–168).
Zeff, Stephen A. K. and Gala G. Dharan (eds) (1994), *Readings
  and Notes on Financial Accounting*, New York: McGraw Hill,
  4th edn, especially chs 1 and 2 (pp. 1–130).

ABOUT THE IEA

The Institute is a research and educational charity (No. CC 235 351), limited by guarantee. Its mission is to improve understanding of the fundamental institutions of a free society with particular reference to the role of markets in solving economic and social problems.

The IEA achieves its mission by:

- a high-quality publishing programme
- conferences, seminars, lectures and other events
- outreach to school and college students
- brokering media introductions and appearances

The IEA, which was established in 1955 by the late Sir Antony Fisher, is an educational charity, not a political organisation. It is independent of any political party or group and does not carry on activities intended to affect support for any political party or candidate in any election or referendum, or at any other time. It is financed by sales of publications, conference fees and voluntary donations.

In addition to its main series of publications the IEA also publishes a quarterly journal, *Economic Affairs*, and has two specialist programmes – Environment and Technology, and Education.

The IEA is aided in its work by a distinguished international Academic Advisory Council and an eminent panel of Honorary Fellows. Together with other academics, they review prospective IEA publications, their comments being passed on anonymously to authors. All IEA papers are therefore subject to the same rigorous independent refereeing process as used by leading academic journals.

IEA publications enjoy widespread classroom use and course adoptions in schools and universities. They are also sold throughout the world and often translated/reprinted.

Since 1974 the IEA has helped to create a world-wide network of 100 similar institutions in over 70 countries. They are all independent but share the IEA's mission.

Views expressed in the IEA's publications are those of the authors, not those of the Institute (which has no corporate view), its Managing Trustees, Academic Advisory Council members or senior staff.

Members of the Institute's Academic Advisory Council, Honorary Fellows, Trustees and Staff are listed on the following page.

The Institute gratefully acknowledges financial support for its publications programme and other work from a generous benefaction by the late Alec and Beryl Warren.

197

Other papers recently published by the IEA include:

WHO, What and Why?

Transnational Government, Legitimacy and the World Health Organization
Roger Scruton
Occasional Paper 113; ISBN 0 255 36487 3
£8.00

The World Turned Rightside Up

A New Trading Agenda for the Age of Globalisation
John C. Hulsman
Occasional Paper 114; ISBN 0 255 36495 4
£8.00

The Representation of Business in English Literature

Introduced and edited by Arthur Pollard
Readings 53; ISBN 0 255 36491 1
£12.00

Anti-Liberalism 2000

The Rise of New Millennium Collectivism
David Henderson
Occasional Paper 115; ISBN 0 255 36497 0
£7.50

Capitalism, Morality and Markets

Brian Griffiths, Robert A. Sirico, Norman Barry & Frank Field
Readings 54; ISBN 0 255 36496 2
£7.50

A Conversation with Harris and Seldon

Ralph Harris & Arthur Seldon
Occasional Paper 116; ISBN 0 255 36498 9
£7.50

Malaria and the DDT Story

Richard Tren & Roger Bate
Occasional Paper 117; ISBN 0 255 36499 7
£10.00

A Plea to Economists Who Favour Liberty: Assist the Everyman

Daniel B. Klein
Occasional Paper 118; ISBN 0 255 36501 2
£10.00

Waging the War of Ideas

John Blundell
Occasional Paper 119; ISBN 0 255 36500 4
£10.00

The Changing Fortunes of Economic Liberalism

Yesterday, Today and Tomorrow
David Henderson
Occasional Paper 105 (new edition); ISBN 0 255 36520 9
£12.50

The Global Education Industry

Lessons from Private Education in Developing Countries
James Tooley
Hobart Paper 141 (new edition); ISBN 0 255 36503 9
£12.50

Saving Our Streams

The Role of the Anglers' Conservation Association in
Protecting English and Welsh Rivers
Roger Bate
Research Monograph 53; ISBN 0 255 36494 6
£10.00

Better Off Out?

The Benefits or Costs of EU Membership
Brian Hindley & Martin Howe
Occasional Paper 99 (new edition); ISBN 0 255 36502 0
£10.00

Buckingham at 25

Freeing the Universities from State Control
Edited by James Tooley
Readings 55; ISBN 0 255 36512 8
£15.00

Lectures on Regulatory and Competition Policy

Irwin M. Stelzer
Occasional Paper 120; ISBN 0 255 36511 X
£12.50

Misguided Virtue

False Notions of Corporate Social Responsibility
David Henderson
Hobart Paper 142; ISBN 0 255 36510 1
£12.50

HIV and Aids in Schools

The Political Economy of Pressure Groups and Miseducation
Barrie Craven, Pauline Dixon, Gordon Stewart & James Tooley
Occasional Paper 121; ISBN 0 255 36522 5
£10.00

The Road to Serfdom

The Reader's Digest *condensed version*
Friedrich A. Hayek
Occasional Paper 122; ISBN 0 255 36530 6
£7.50

Bastiat's *The Law*

Introduction by Norman Barry
Occasional Paper 123; ISBN 0 255 36509 8
£7.50

A Globalist Manifesto for Public Policy

Charles Calomiris
Occasional Paper 124; ISBN 0 255 36525 X
£7.50

Euthanasia for Death Duties

Putting Inheritance Tax Out of Its Misery
Barry Bracewell-Milnes
Research Monograph 54; ISBN 0 255 36513 6
£10.00

Liberating the Land
The Case for Private Land-use Planning
Mark Pennington
Hobart Paper 143; ISBN 0 255 36508 X
£10.00

IEA Yearbook of Government Performance 2002/2003
Edited by Peter Warburton
Yearbook 1; ISBN 0 255 36532 2
£15.00

Britain's Relative Economic Performance, 1870–1999
Nicholas Crafts
Research Monograph 55; ISBN 0 255 36524 1
£10.00

Should We Have Faith in Central Banks?
Otmar Issing
Occasional Paper 125; ISBN 0 255 36528 4
£7.50

The Dilemma of Democracy

Arthur Seldon

Hobart Paper 136 (reissue); ISBN 0 255 36536 5

£10.00

Capital Controls: a 'Cure' Worse Than the Problem?

Forrest Capie

Research Monograph 56; ISBN 0 255 36506 3

£10.00

The Poverty of 'Development Economics'

Deepak Lal

Hobart Paper 144 (reissue); ISBN 0 255 36519 5

£15.00

Should Britain Join the Euro?

The Chancellor's Five Tests Examined

Patrick Minford

Occasional Paper 126; ISBN 0 255 36527 6

£7.50

Post-Communist Transition: Some Lessons

Leszek Balcerowicz

Occasional Paper 127; ISBN 0 255 36533 0

£7.50

A Tribute to Peter Bauer

John Blundell et al.
Occasional Paper 128; ISBN 0 255 36531 4
£10.00

Employment Tribunals

Their Growth and the Case for Radical Reform
J. R. Shackleton
Hobart Paper 145; ISBN 0 255 36515 2
£10.00

Fifty Economic Fallacies Exposed

Geoffrey E. Wood
Occasional Paper 129; ISBN 0 255 36518 7
£12.50

A Market in Airport Slots

Keith Boyfield (editor), David Starkie, Tom Bass & Barry Humphreys
Readings 56; ISBN 0 255 36505 5
£10.00

Money, Inflation and the Constitutional Position of the Central Bank

Milton Friedman & Charles A. E. Goodhart
Readings 57; ISBN 0 255 36538 1
£10.00

railway.com

Parallels between the early British railways and the ICT revolution

Robert C. B. Miller

Research Monograph 57; ISBN 0 255 36534 9

£12.50

The Regulation of Financial Markets

Edited by Philip Booth & David Currie

Readings 58; ISBN 0 255 36551 9

£12.50

Climate Alarmism Reconsidered

Robert L. Bradley Jr

Hobart Paper 146; ISBN 0 255 36541 1

£12.50

Government Failure: E. G. West on Education

Edited by James Tooley & James Stanfield

Occasional Paper 130; ISBN 0 255 36552 7

£12.50

Waging the War of Ideas

John Blundell

Second edition

Occasional Paper 131; ISBN 0 255 36547 0

£12.50

Corporate Governance: Accountability in the Marketplace

Elaine Sternberg
Second edition
Hobart Paper 147; ISBN 0 255 36542 X
£12.50

The Land Use Planning System

Evaluating Options for Reform
John Corkindale
Hobart Paper 148; ISBN 0 255 36550 0
£10.00

Economy and Virtue

Essays on the Theme of Markets and Morality
Edited by Dennis O'Keeffe
Readings 59; ISBN 0 255 36504 7
£12.50

Free Markets Under Siege

Cartels, Politics and Social Welfare
Richard A. Epstein
Occasional Paper 132; ISBN 0 255 36553 5
£10.00

To order copies of currently available IEA papers, or to enquire about availability, please contact:

Lavis Marketing
IEA orders
FREEPOST LON21280
Oxford OX3 7BR

Tel: 01865 767575
Fax: 01865 750079
Email: orders@lavismarketing.co.uk

The IEA also offers a subscription service to its publications. For a single annual payment, currently £40.00 in the UK, you will receive every title the IEA publishes across the course of a year, invitations to events, and discounts on our extensive back catalogue. For more information, please contact:

Subscriptions
The Institute of Economic Affairs
2 Lord North Street
London SW1P 3LB

Tel: 020 7799 8900
Fax: 020 7799 2137
Website: www.iea.org.uk